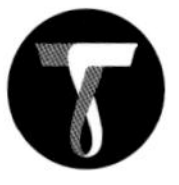

TROPE PUBLISHING Co.

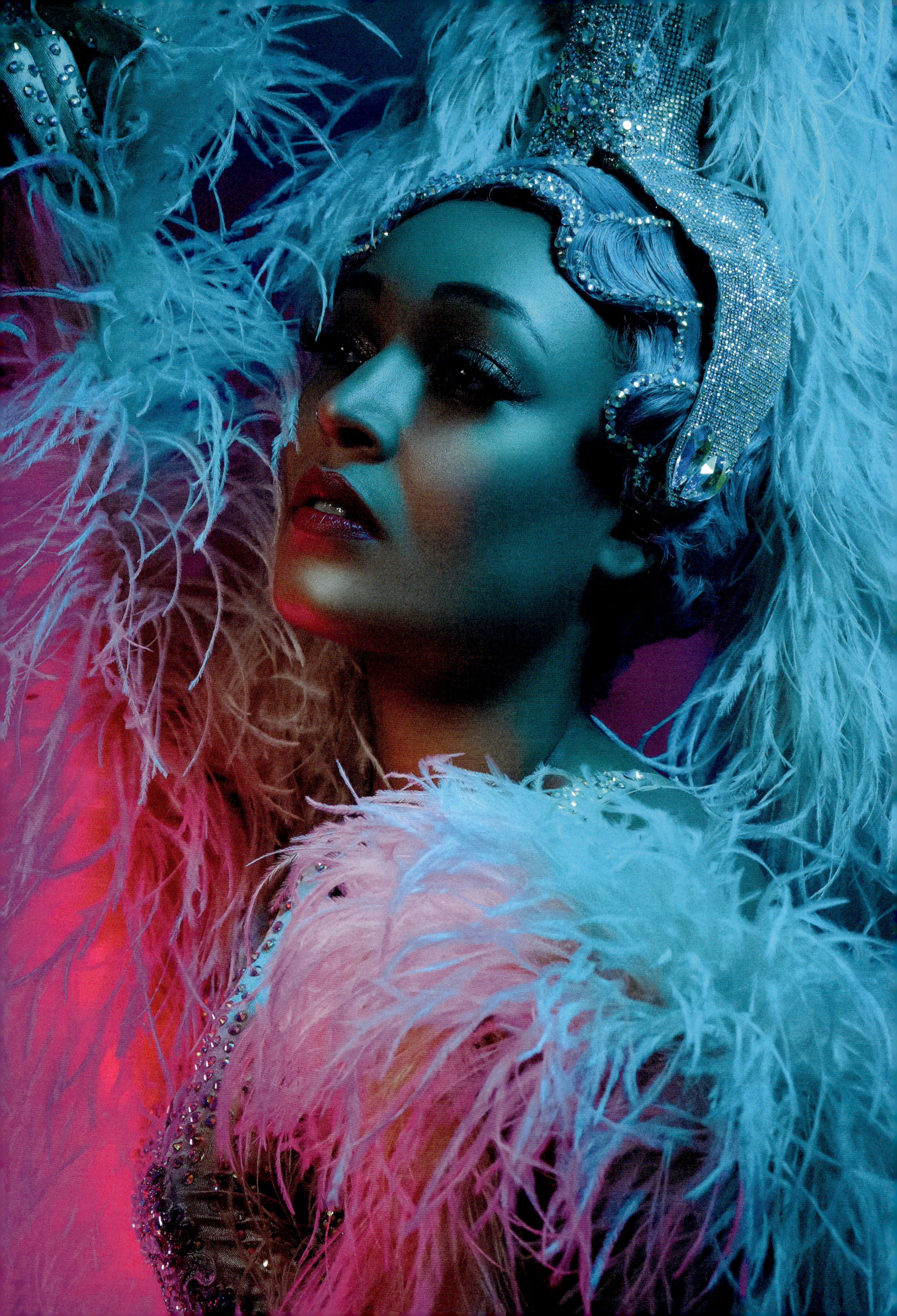

# LIFE AS A CABARET

## A MODERN PORTRAIT

Photographs by

**VERONIKA MARX**

Text by

**MARK ANTHONY**

# FOREWORD

If we move past the absurdity of me writing the foreword to a book of any description. If we forget for one second that an Australian comedian writing the foreword to a book is like asking a mule to paint the Sistine Chapel or an American football player to find the square root of pi. If we simply forget that, then really this is fitting.

I began my career and, in fact, my childhood to cabaret. Not the film by Bob Fosse, the horror of every last-minute Halloween costume or birthday theme. Not the common idea of cabaret you've seen on *Britain's Got Talent*—"That's too…cabaret" we hear yet again. But real cabaret: dirty, political, current, and angry. My parents were communists who took me to meetings as a child. I still remember mugging my way through "The Internationale" and thinking of the subsequent trip to the butcher's where I'd get a whole kabana sausage to myself to keep me quiet. Looking back on this, I'm answering a lot of questions.

But I'm getting distracted. I'm here to write the foreword for Veronika Marx and Mark Anthony's literary venture, *Life as a Cabaret*.

Cabaret gets a bad rep up and down the rungs of the arts hierarchy. Admittedly, most of that is due to me, but it is my favourite art form because it can encapsulate, utilise, and smash together any and every discipline. In fact, to be called cabaret, to be classified as this impure gutter art, it *must* include them. It's a mutt, and maybe that's why it is so beloved and has stuck to the consciousness of our society for so long. A mutt lives longer than a purebred. It's a subversion of the ingredients that make it up. It's an immature middle finger up at its own artistic parents and at society's expectations, mores, social codes, systems, and definitions.

Cabaret is punk. It is nihilism.

In this tome, Mark and Veronika capture that dreaded word: demimonde. Why? I have no idea, as they famously have no money, but that may be the point. To capture the rejection of luxury via the performance of glamour by those society feels aren't deserving. Mark and Veronika are aiming their lens at true cabaret, rather than the sanitised, candied ideal we see on our TVs in the current explosion of drag. And that is not to say that the world discovering it isn't a wonderful thing, but for an entire population to find subversion in any form appealing, it requires that art form to sand off its edges and smooth its corners. And suddenly, the subversion of a social more ends up becoming obedient acquiescence. Especially when it plays a part in capitalism as opposed to throwing a spanner in the gears.

Cabaret is a party, but true cabaret is a riot. And riots are fought first by those on the fringes of society, by the most vulnerable. By people who are queer, trans, disabled, and non-white. It's been documented how gay liberation is owed to these people. How ballroom culture, now worldwide in its appeal—stomping Madonna's, Beyonce's, and even Taylor Swift's global tours—was founded by Black and Latinx queer communities. How queerness itself survived organised religion's attempts to stamp it out. The people on the edges create a culture out of necessity. Those in the centre use it as a hashtag, such is the way of the world. *Life as a Cabaret* pays tribute to and captures those who create culture.

Both Mark and Veronika have become a mainstay in the European cabaret industry. Veronika by capturing on her lens burlesque and circus artists from all over the globe and Mark by ruling over the pubs, the gutter bars, the garages, and warehouses. Veronika's signature feminine, beautiful style and Mark's gritty, bawdy, politicised mega masculinity combine glamour and rage with vulnerability and humour. In this book, there is laid bare before you, not just an industry, but a community—a family. Every one of us and our bodies, faces, and lives that society has pushed to the edge, who all live on a precipice and who sadly in the rampant rise of conservatism, are becoming endangered. We have constructed identities, personas, and characters not just as armour, but to create a new world.

I believe that drag, cabaret—any art form that comes directly from the creator and is performed by the creator—is a form of terraforming. It is escapism for both the audience and the artist because in that moment the artist is building the world they want to see and can live in, brick by brick by brick. People think of cabaret artists as wine-soaked, sardonic, curmudgeons, but a pessimist is just an optimist with standards. We are stonemasons of the new world, yet we have always been here. And more importantly, we're not going anywhere.

I hope you enjoy this book. I hope you love it as much as we have enjoyed providing the content. More than that, I hope when you look at it you see possibility and not consequence. I hope you see joy but also the anger. I hope you see the courage and the love. The love that each of these artists has for their art and for the world they're building right in front of you.

Now, I have to go. There's a twink in my dressing room who's not getting any fresher.

Sadly, that twink is me.

**REUBEN KAYE**

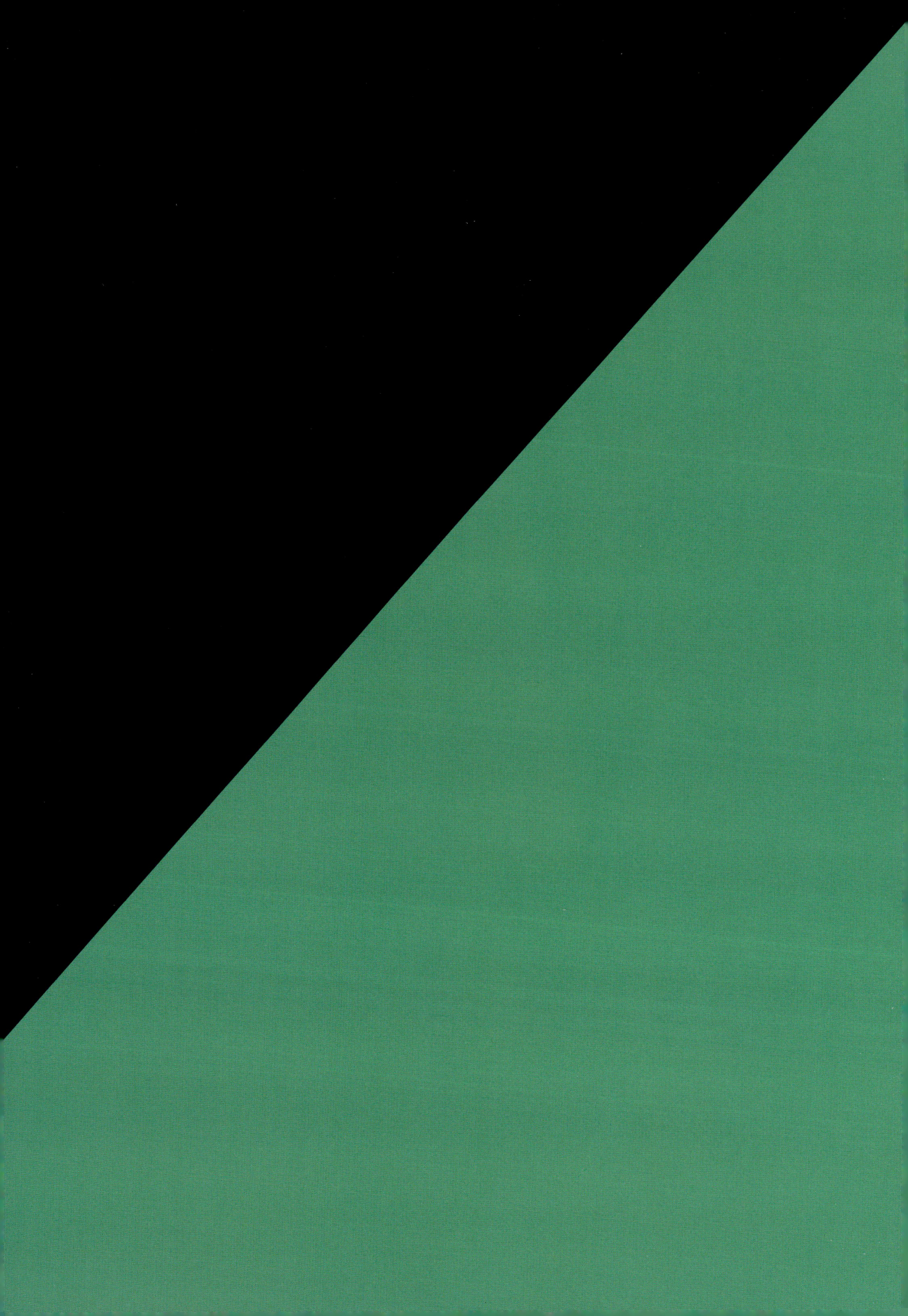

# INTRODUCTION

Cabaret has historically existed on the fringes of society, populated by those who find themselves, voluntarily or involuntarily, falling outside of the conventional. It pushes the boundaries of gender, politics, identity, power, and social norms. It's live and unpredictable, bringing together a variety of performances to create a unique, and often never-repeated, entertainment experience. Typically, a cabaret show consists of a selection of short acts hosted by a compère, with performers demonstrating a variety of styles and genres, which today would most commonly include drag, burlesque, boylesque, circus, and sideshow. Shows happen anywhere and everywhere—bar, club, theatre, library, carpark. Cabaret's adaptability and ephemeral nature are what set it apart from the formality and precision of traditional theatre.

Since 2016 I've been working full-time as a cabaret performer. I am a Drag King, Boylesque performer, occasional vocalist, and compère. I'm also queer, trans, and non-binary, a fact that, for better or worse, is intricately linked to my career. Performing professionally was never the plan. Since I can remember, I was determined to be the next Indiana Jones. I went to university and studied archaeology, believing after graduation I'd spend my days digging up the Earth, but unfortunately, things didn't pan out that way. The struggle to find a job and the unexpected development of a rare eyesight condition left me rethinking my life plan. I moved to London, hoping like so many others before me that the big city would provide the answers, but all I seemed to encounter were barriers. I stumbled through a series of jobs, but I couldn't find a place where I could be successful and authentically myself. What I did find in London, however, was an amazing queer community.

When I first began going to drag shows, I had an idea of what drag was from what I'd seen on television, but the performances I saw in London were nothing like it. My very first experience was at the legendary cabaret venue, The Royal Vauxhall Tavern, at Bar Wotever, which was a weekly evening show where newcomers could book a spot with very few questions asked. There was also a rotating cast of more established performers hosting and trying out new acts, so as an audience member, you never knew what you were going to see. My eyes were quickly opened to a huge, baffling world of creativity that I'd never experienced before.

I became obsessed with Drag Kings, and found Boi Box, a monthly Drag King cabaret in the heart of Soho. I was still in the early stages of untangling my own web of gender and sexuality, and watching Drag Kings perform helped me make sense of things. It wasn't enough to just be an audience member though, so in a moment of foolish bravery, I volunteered for an open mic slot at Bar Wotever. I had no stage name and I'd never even performed by myself before. A voice inside my head was telling me I had absolutely no business being on that stage, but I knew it was something I needed to do.

My first performance was unspectacular to say the least. I sang a Bruce Springsteen song in extremely basic drag, with dodgy makeup and not a rhinestone in sight. At that time, it felt hugely transgressive to even walk into the men's section of Primark, so the costume that was in reality a pair of black jeans and a white t-shirt felt to me like a mind-blowing transformation. Ultimately though, none of those elements of the performance were relevant. What truly mattered was how it felt: the anxiety of waiting backstage and questioning every life decision that led me to that moment, the heat of the lights on my face when I walked through the velvet curtains, the gnaw of terror in my stomach just before I croaked out the first few hesitant notes and the shock of my voice echoing through a microphone. Half of me never wanted to do it again, and the other half was immediately looking for the next opportunity to.

Eight years later and cabaret is my entire life.

I love the freedom of creating for a living and the feeling of accomplishment that comes with being responsible for your successes. I love the backstage atmospheres, the jokes and support, the sharing of wig glue and makeup, and sewing people into their costumes when they break. I love the collective joy of putting on a great show and the commiseration when something goes wrong. I quickly learnt that outside of our own community, opportunities for Drag Kings, and trans-masculine performers in general, were extremely rare. I've learned the hard way that getting that respect is an endless uphill battle, and I've also learned that it's a lifestyle that can be draining and unhealthy. When your career success is based on endless self-promotion, it's easy to lose touch with who you are off stage, and every setback can feel like a personal attack. Finding the balance is tough, but every time I step on stage all those difficulties just seem to melt away. There's an element of escapism in the instability and a sense of belonging, an unspoken understanding that can be and is a beautiful lifeline for many.

This book is not only a cross-section of this world, but also a love letter to it. We've taken the performers from the stage lights to a studio light, to showcase their individuality as works of art in and of themselves. We wanted to immortalise the beauty and power of these individuals who are determined to stand out from the crowd, embracing the hustle, oddness, contradictions, differences, and most of all, the unstoppable creativity.

*Life as a Cabaret* celebrates and highlights the vibrancy and diversity of the underground cabaret scene, uplifting and representing those who are typically overlooked. It showcases this incredibly dynamic and fascinating world for what it really is: glamorous, polished, and professional certainly, but also intoxicatingly punk, inescapably queer, and gloriously messy. It's a space for experimentation, for pushing and challenging boundaries, for seeking a voice and a platform—creating dystopias and eutopias, even just for one night.

## MARK ANTHONY

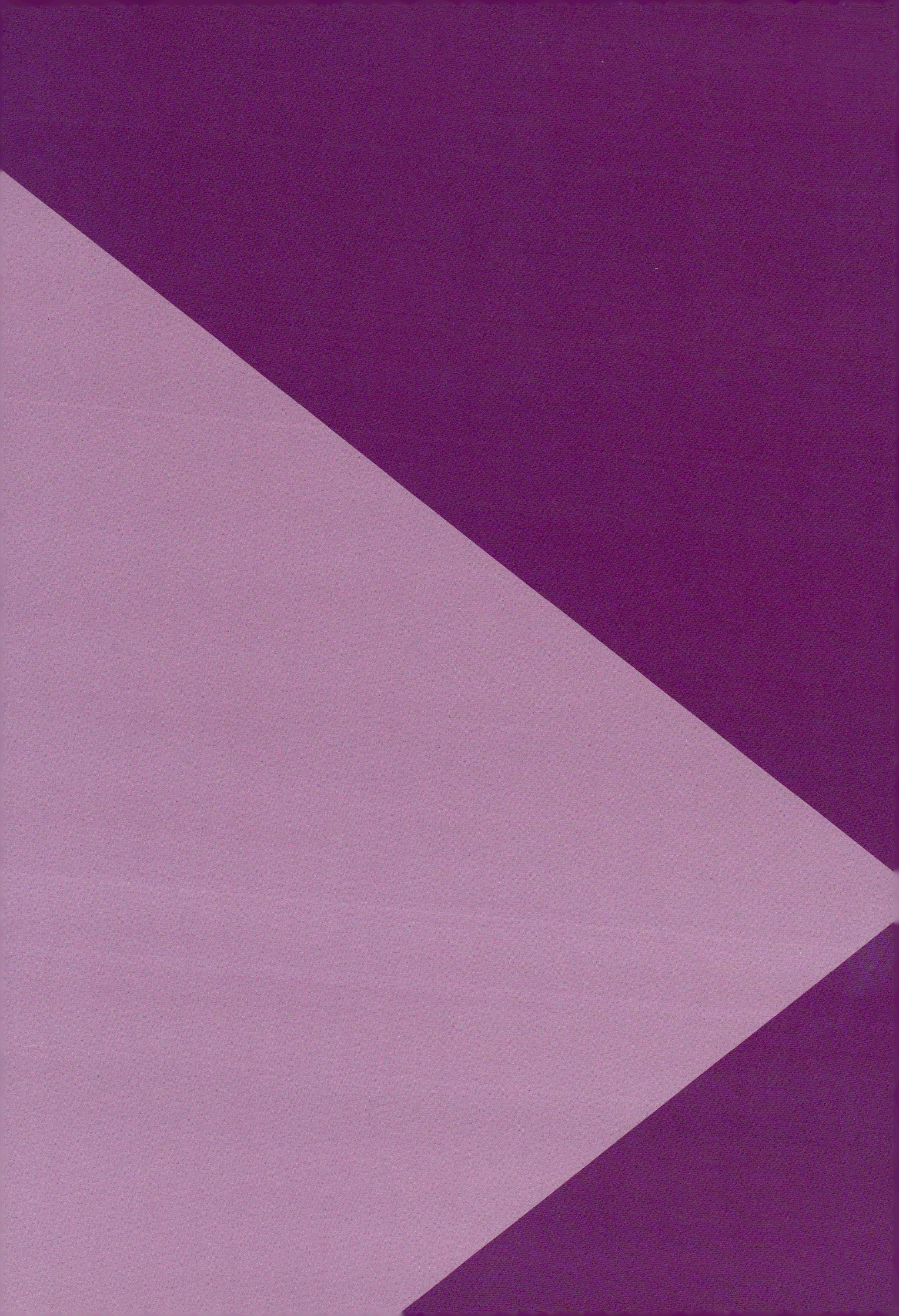

# PERFORMANCE GENRES

## DRAG KING

A Drag King is someone who performs masculinity, whether as a critique, a form of self-expression, a political statement, a character choice, or all the above in a variety of combinations. Although historically tied to the lesbian community, Drag Kings can be women, trans men, non-binary, or even cis men, with the majority of professional Kings falling under the trans, trans-masculine, or non-binary umbrellas.

Drag Kings, formerly known as "male impersonators," can trace their history back at least several hundred years. During the golden age of music halls in the Victorian period and even up to World War II, some Drag Kings, like Vesta Tilley, were household names. Tilley and others such as Hetty King, Annie Hindle, and Ella Shields were well-paid entertainers that toured the UK and United States to great acclaim and sold-out theatres. They also performed for royalty as they became firm fixtures of the cabaret scene.

While Tilley was, as far as we know, heterosexual and married to a man who wrote many of her songs, other male impersonators like Annie Hindle were more or less openly queer. Male impersonation allowed many performers to express queerness and gender fluidity in their everyday lives to a much greater extent than was generally acceptable in society.

As time went on, male impersonation outside of traditional theatre became increasingly associated with queerness and gender transgression, and perhaps for that reason, dropped increasingly off the radar.

Though struggling to gain platforms of the same magnitude as their Drag Queen siblings, Drag Kings are still very much a part of the cabaret scene. In contrast to their predecessors, most Kings now perform under masculine stage names. There are a very small number of Drag Kings performing full-time. This is mostly due to a substantial pay gap and the difficulty of finding consistent work during a time when the demand for drag entertainment is at an all-time high, but the type of drag that producers and often audiences are willing to invest in is narrow.

Many people are still unaware of Drag Kings, however, in the last few years they have been gaining visibility, proving in many cases that their absence is not due to a lack of quality, but opportunity.

# DRAG QUEEN

There is an assumption that a Drag Queen is a man dressed as a woman, especially since there is a myth that the origin of the term "Drag" was first used as an acronym for "dressed as a girl" during the Shakespearean era. It indicated that a male actor would be dressed in women's clothing, though at this time, all actors were male. A true definition requires nuance.

With our language surrounding gender evolving, the reality is there are many Drag Queens who are women, non-binary, or trans. Being a Drag Queen isn't ultimately determined by identity off-stage but rather the type of character one occupies on stage, which is usually centred in exaggerated or performative femininity.

Sometimes divided into the "old school" and "new school," old school drag queens are associated with dramatic, often garish, makeup, extravagant outfits, live vocals, and a brutal wit. New school Drag Queens retain many of these features but with a greater emphasis on lip-syncs, movement, dancing, and tricks like the infamous death drop.

Drag Queens have long been present in popular culture, with names like Divine, Lily Savage, RuPaul, and Dame Edna being familiar to most. They are sources of humour, known to speak freely and act in defiance of social graces that other entertainment personalities could not get away with. They hold a central place in the queer community and are often looked to as leaders, both in entertainment and in the fight for civil rights.

Although there have always been many other types of people involved in these struggles, it has often been the case that Drag Queens and trans women become the face of them, and consequently bear much of the backlash. The rise in popularity of drag has also opened it up to attack, perhaps because a male-dominated society fears the power of femininity. In the UK and even more so in the United States, drag performers are finding themselves at the centre of volatile political and social debates as society struggles to reconcile itself with changing understandings of gender and sexuality.

Despite that, it is fair to say that Drag Queens are more popular now than ever before, finding mainstream success and unprecedented opportunities for fame and fortune.

# BURLESQUE

To a modern audience, burlesque is the art of striptease, seduction, and performative sexuality. Performances can be divided into two categories: classical burlesque—which includes fan dances, bump and grind, showgirl aesthetics, richly decorated and refined costumes with an emphasis on movement and tease—and neo-burlesque—which has more modern references and music, is often comedic or overtly political, and displays a broader style of costumes and movement.

Historically, burlesque has commonly been performed by cisgender women, however, there is an increasingly diverse range of performers including trans women, non-binary people and even cis men. Although rooted firmly in the empowerment of women, much like drag, burlesque truly refers to a style of performance that can be performed by anyone.

The origin of burlesque can be traced back to the 17th century when it was derived from Italian words meaning "joke" or "mockery." In the Victorian era in the UK, it was used to describe a satirical show featuring an all-female chorus line, which parodied popular opera and theatre of the time. These shows were also referred to as a Travesty or Extravaganza, and were radical in their empowerment of female performers. In the 1800s, these shows arrived in the US. Lydia Thompson and her troupe, the British Blondes, who arrived in New York in 1868, are largely credited with the popularising of burlesque in the US, and what made them particularly revolutionary was that their productions were entirely written and produced by women.

The element of striptease didn't emerge fully until the 20th century. In the 1920s, large performance companies formed in the US, mirrored by the peak of legendary Parisian chorus lines like Folies Bergere and the Moulin Rouge. The 1930s saw a greater focus on solo performers and revues, making way for some of the most well-known burlesque names, including Josephine Baker, whose iconic "danse sauvage" with banana skirt and slicked down hair, a powerful parody of racial stereotypes, propelled her to fame.

In the UK, burlesque, along with many other mainstays of Victorian music hall, began to see a decline in popularity from the 1890s, replaced by more wholesome forms of Edwardian entertainment. A similar decline occurred in the US from the 1940s largely thanks to the restrictions and censorship imposed on the New York scene. In both cases, burlesque certainly did not disappear, merely shifting out of mainstream entertainment venues and theatres and into nightlife spaces.

Burlesque saw a major rebirth in the 1990s with the emergence of performers like Dirty Martini, Pearl Noire, and Dita Von Teese.

# BOYLESQUE

Unlike its drag and burlesque peers, boylesque as a term is a relatively new phenomenon, possibly finding its origins in 1960s Hollywood. Originally coined as a term to place this style of performance somewhere between traditionally female burlesque and Chippendales-style male revue, it usually describes a male-identified artist or someone appearing as a male character performing acts centred around striptease and storytelling in a style similar to burlesque.

While boylesque and burlesque can easily be grouped under the same umbrella, boylesque performers often use the term to separate themselves from burlesque out of respect for burlesque's history of female empowerment and to emphasize its focus on the performance of masculinity rather than femininity. For each genre, the flow of the tease is usually dictated by the body parts of the performer which are most sexualised.

Boylesque-style performers were present in the 1880s, notably Henry Dixey, who was famous for his comedic "Adonis" act, although much like burlesque of the time, this did not involve stripping. In the 1890s, bodybuilder Eugen Sandow, a protege of Florenz Ziegfeld, was known for performing nude except for a fig leaf. During the 1920s, boylesque acts were more commonly found in the queer, underground scenes of Paris and Berlin. One popular figure was Hubert Julian Stowitts, who danced nearly nude for the Folies Bergère in Paris.

The word boylesque or "boylesk" began to be more widely used to describe these kinds of performances in the 1960s and 70s. Throughout the history of boylesque, acts have explored the gentler elements of masculinity as well as its fluidity with femininity, some sitting more closely in style and aesthetic to burlesque, as well as the other hardened, stereotypical elements of masculinity, with a focus on physical strength and a muscular physique that align more closely with the Chippendales-style male revue.

Although it remains a significantly smaller scene than burlesque, boylesque has steadily increased in popularity since its conception. Most performers of this genre are now based in the US, where it finds its greatest popularity, including its own category at the renowned Burlesque Hall of Fame until 2023, when the categories were combined into one competition. However, an international scene does exist. Though small, it is growing, and seeing increasing crossover with the Drag King community.

# QUEERLESQUE

The term "queer," as it is most used today, is simply the description of a sexual or gender identity that falls outside of what society sees as the norm. It's a word that historically has been a derogatory slur, and which has been almost universally rehabilitated as a term of pride and community identity. Queerlesque is a term that it is difficult to trace the origins of, although anecdotally it seems to have come into use in the last decade. For some, it is an add-on to burlesque or boylesque, a word used to describe the queer influences in some of their acts. For others, it describes their style of performance and is a way to find space between the two genres which allows for a freer expression of gender. It is also used to describe the increasing incorporation of drag into burlesque and boylesque. While cabaret and drag shows have always been predominantly queer spaces, at least from the performers' side of things, burlesque has become more explicitly linked to the queer community in recent years.

Burlesque has always been political. While it is an art form with elements that now seem to harken back to a bygone era, in many ways it has always been and remains a reflection of the struggles for freedom of the time. Art forms rooted in satire are inherently topical—they hold a mirror up to society—and burlesque has always pushed the limits of what is socially acceptable at any given time.

While it is undeniably rooted in feminism and women's empowerment, burlesque has continued to push at the limits of what's "normal," embracing the exploration of masculinity as another element in the struggle for gender equality and incorporating the fight for visibility and representation of queer performers.

The motivations for performing burlesque are endlessly diverse: whether it's building confidence and self-acceptance, pursuing personal sexual empowerment, or reclaiming the sexualisation forced upon women and their bodies by a patriarchal society. The community of burlesque as a whole works on an ethos of inclusivity, but it cannot escape the beauty standards of the rest of society. Certain burlesque bodies are undeniably more celebrated and accepted than others: cisgender bodies, slim bodies, white bodies, heterosexual bodies, able bodies. These are the bodies that are seen when burlesque enters the mainstream.

The explicit injection of queerness into burlesque is one way of disrupting these beauty standards, upending the assumption that burlesque is about a woman appealing to the sexuality of a man. Queerlesque uplifts those that are usually othered and explores attraction and beauty outside of heterosexuality through queer aesthetics including drag or queer storylines and ideologies.

# NON-BINARY DRAG

Defining non-binary drag is somewhat of an exercise in defining the undefinable. As understanding and vocabulary around gender identity and sexuality has expanded, so has the language used to describe drag performers. If the definitions of Drag King and Drag Queen are boiled down to their most simplistic version, the performance of masculinity and femininity respectively, then non-binary drag can be explained as the performance of gender outside of a male/female binary. It's just one of several terms used by drag performers whose on-stage personas are neither male nor female, or even human. They might also be described as Drag Things or Drag Creatures, among other terms. Non-binary is also a term used outside of drag. In some cases, non-binary individuals also consider themselves to be trans, but many consider it a distinct identity.

Some performers approach their stage personas as separate entities, fully formed characters with their own backstories and personalities. Others will describe their presence on stage as an extension or exaggeration of themselves. When it comes to gender identity, some approach drag as the performance of a gender opposite to their own. Others perform a heightened version of their own gender identity while some choose to occupy a space outside of gender. Some use drag to explore a specific and fixed gender and others explore a more fluid and changeable presentation. Just like we're continuously exploring and questioning the relationships between gender and sexuality as a society, the drag performer and drag persona can be linked and separated in infinitely different ways.

Many of these concepts can be attributed to the Club Kids movement, an influential phenomenon that began in the 1980s and 90s, particularly in the dance, drag, and queer venues of New York and London. The Club Kids were queer drag and performance artists who found themselves disenfranchised even from the dominant drag and gay cultures of the time. They experimented with over-the-top, outlandish fashion and androgynous gender expression, creating extravagant personalities, often carrying an element of notoriety. Perhaps the most well-known example in the UK was Leigh Bowery, fashion icon, artist, and stalwart of London's club scene. In New York, some of the most iconic Club Kids were James St James, Amanda Lepore, and RuPaul. Their looks defied the boundaries of gender, sexuality, practicality, and the human body itself, and their influence can still be seen on some of the biggest fashion runways and music stages.

Although the original Club Kids may not have described themselves using these more modern terms, or even have considered themselves to exist outside the gender binary in their day-to-day lives, non-binary drag artists push at the boundaries of drag in similar ways, developing new styles of makeup, storytelling, costuming, and movement that cross and combine gender expressions.

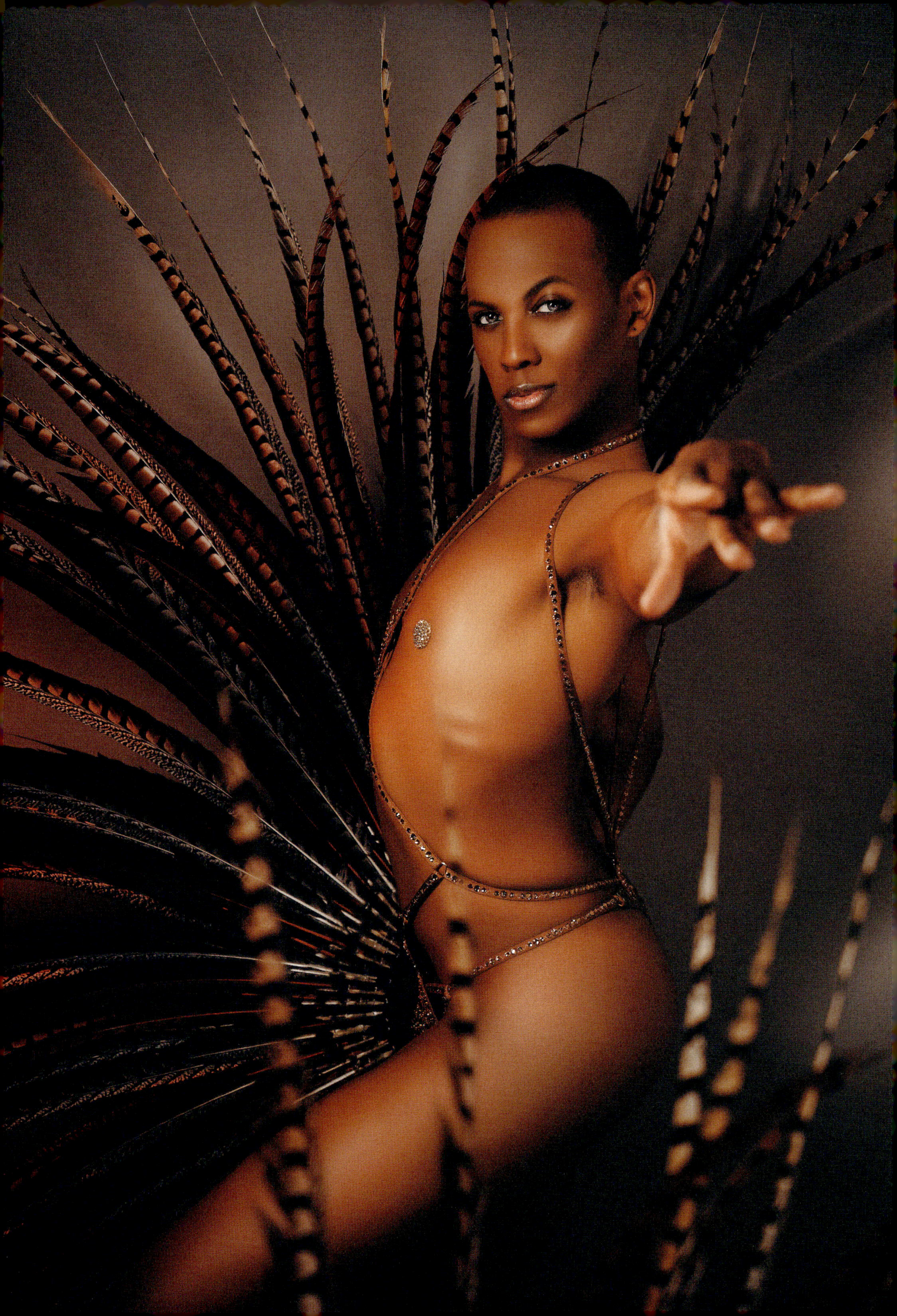

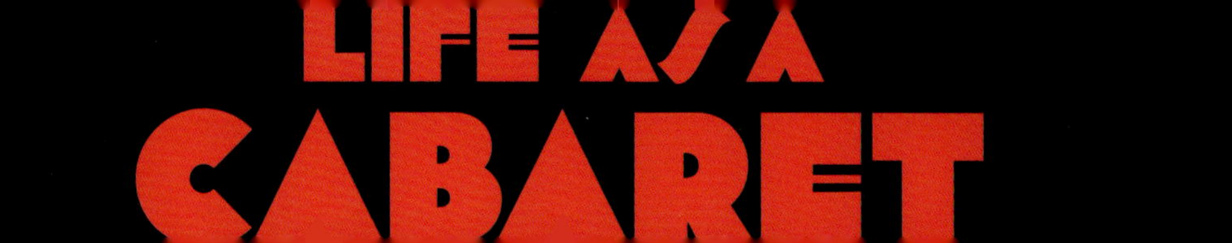

LIFE AS A
CABARET

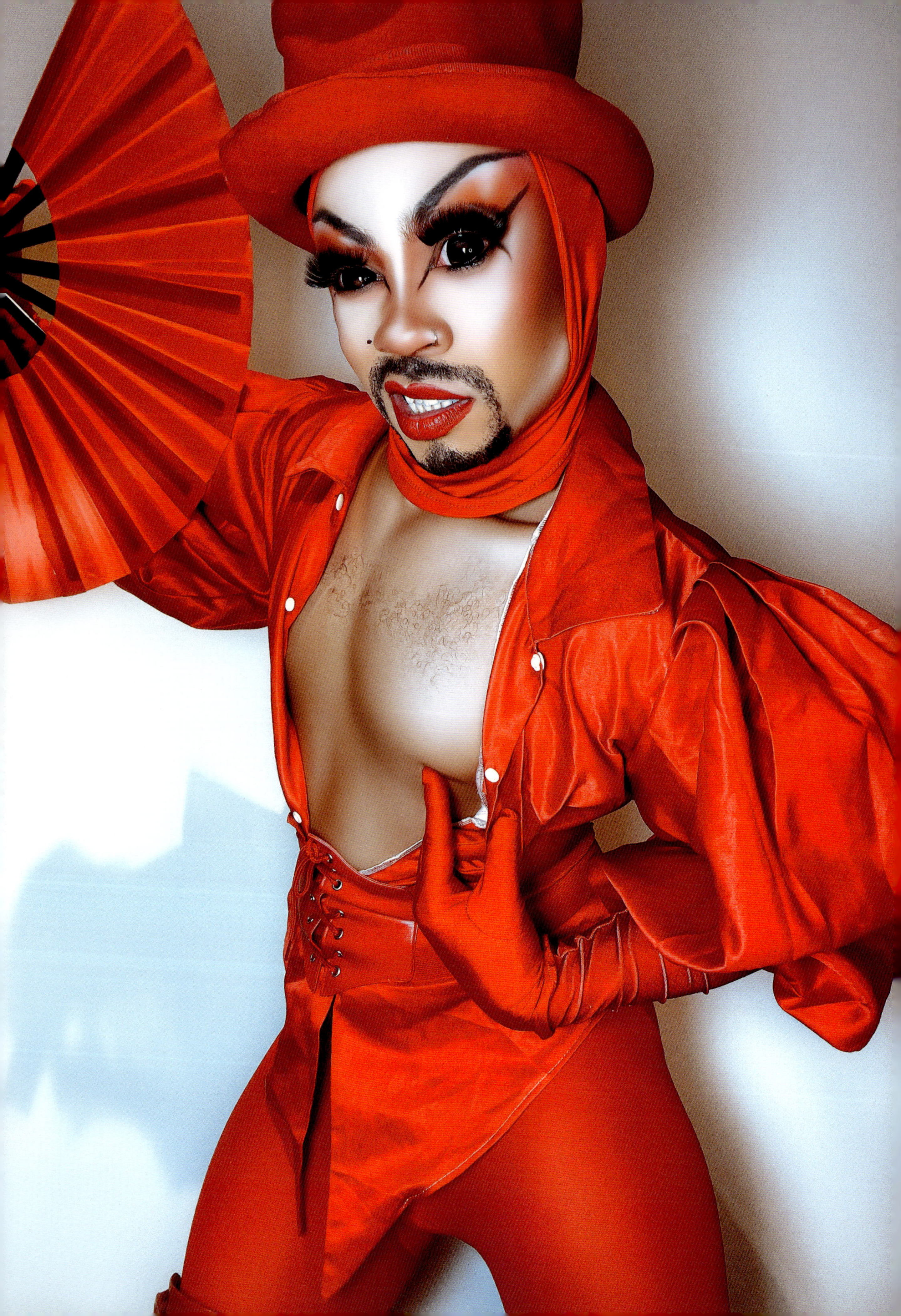

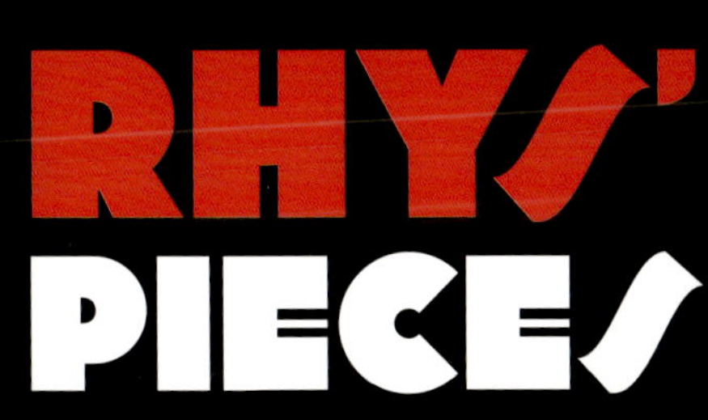

# RHYS' PIECES

## DRAG CREATURE & QUEERLESQUE

Rhys' Pieces is a genderbending drag being and creature. Their art explores the issues of gender, sexuality, identity, and race, creating work that is both political and fun—all the pieces of Rhys. Their performances incorporate the fluidity of their race and gender and are influenced by a love of physical theatre and mythological creatures, both grand and grotesque, as well as playing with the forms of matriarchal dames, clown, and fool.

# BETTY FVCK

## DRAG QUEEN & DRAGLESQUE

Betty Fvck is an international drag and queerlesque performer, originally from Vietnam and now based in Helsinki, Finland. As well as being a lynchpin in the Helsinki cabaret scene, as producer of the Helsinki Queerlesque and Helsinki Drag Festivals, she is also the first Drag Queen in the world to run for parliament, having stood in the Finnish parliamentary elections in 2023.

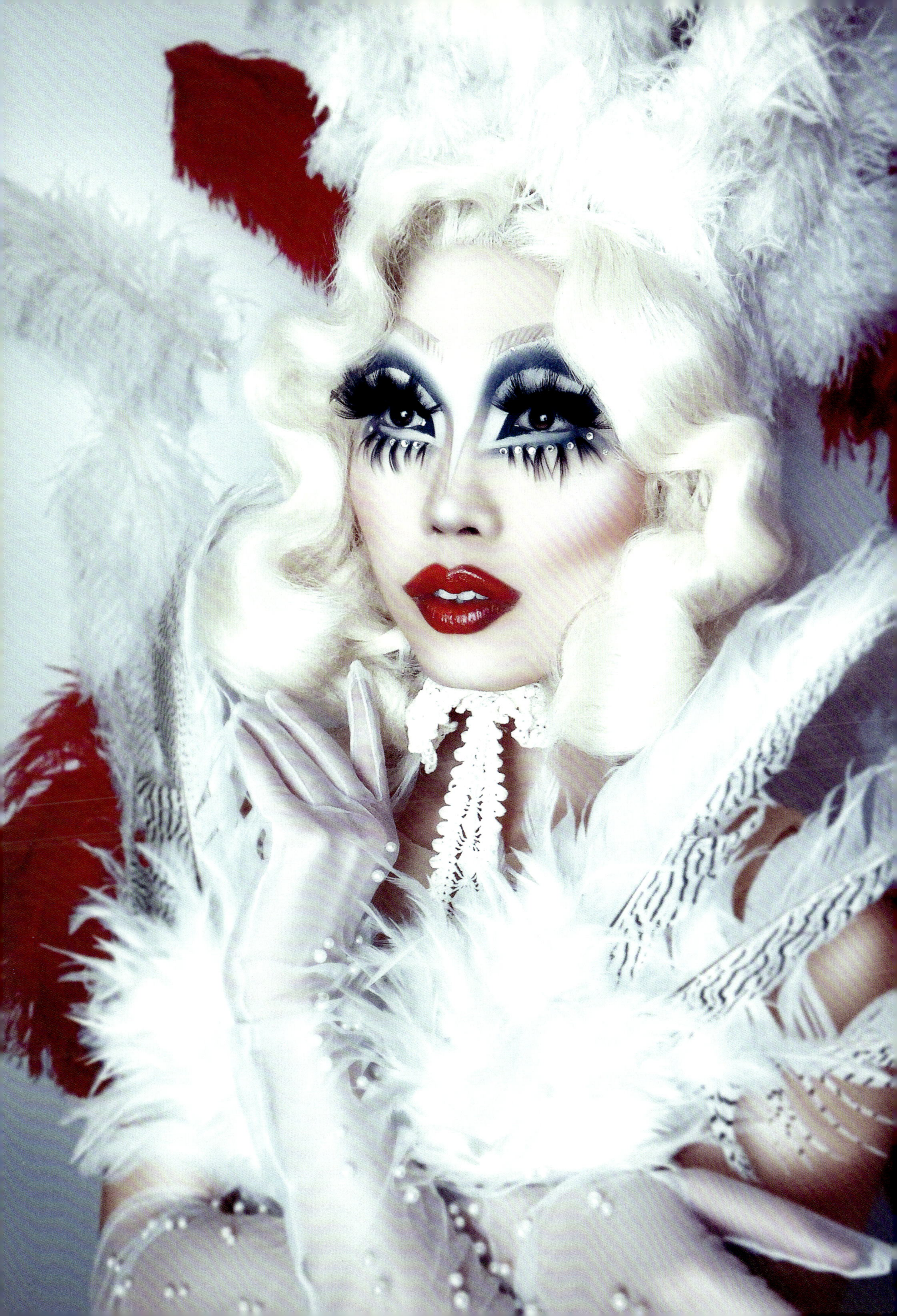

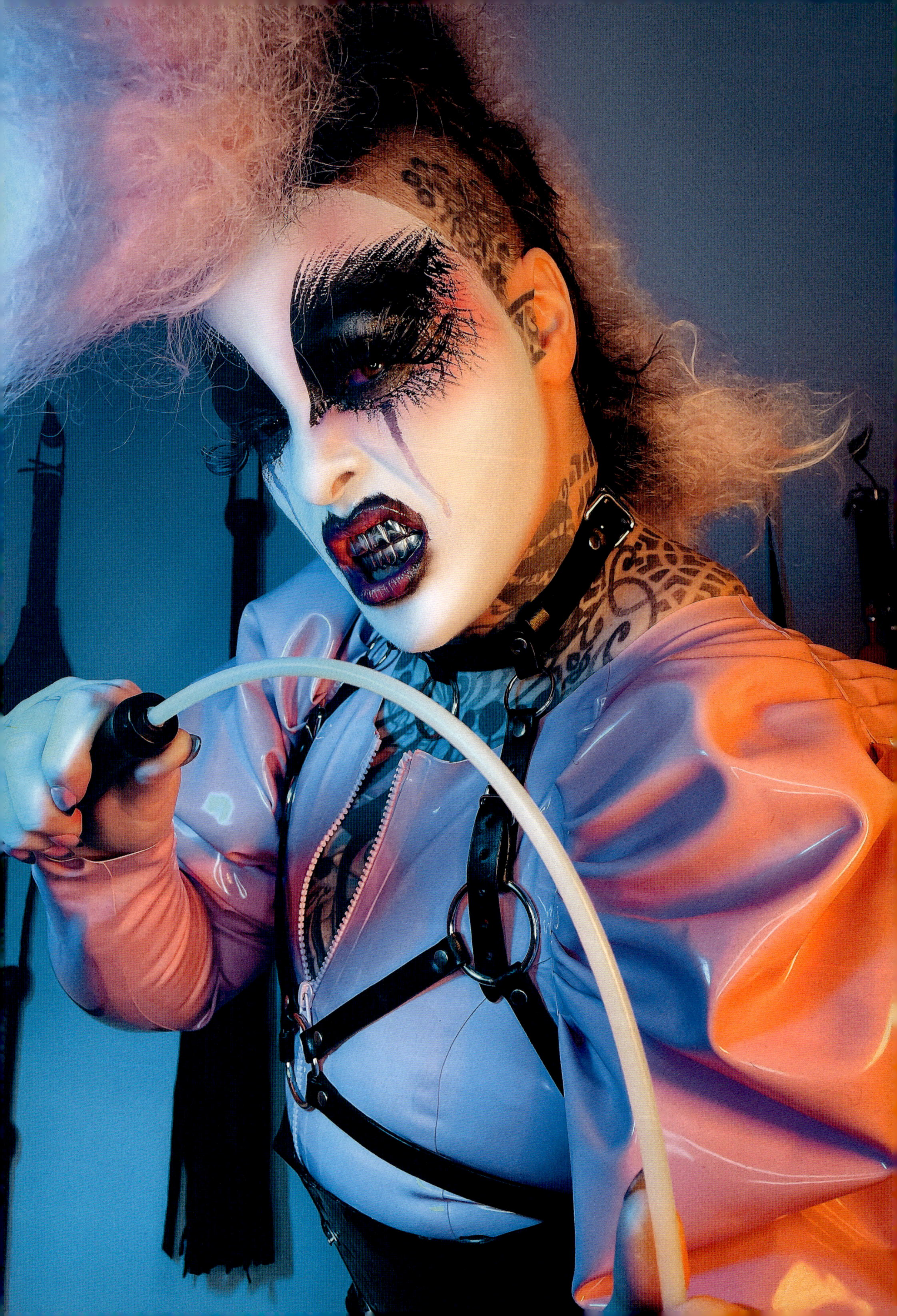

# KING CONFUZA
## DRAG CREATURE & QUEERLESQUE

King Confuza is a 4000-year-old friendly neighbourhood cryptid. He's a gender non-conforming nightmare who loves to blend drag with his favourite horror and cult references. With a killer aesthetic inspired by 1980s goth and new wave fashions, he is often referred to as "The Prince of Thotness," but most people just call him Daddy.

"It's full of energy, art, creativity, adrenaline, endorphins, sweat, glitter, and prosecco."

# CADBURY
# PARFAIT

## BURLESQUE

Cadbury Parfait is a Black, queer, burlesque artist. She's an international and award-winning performer who serves classic burlesque with a hint of British tongue-in-cheek humour.

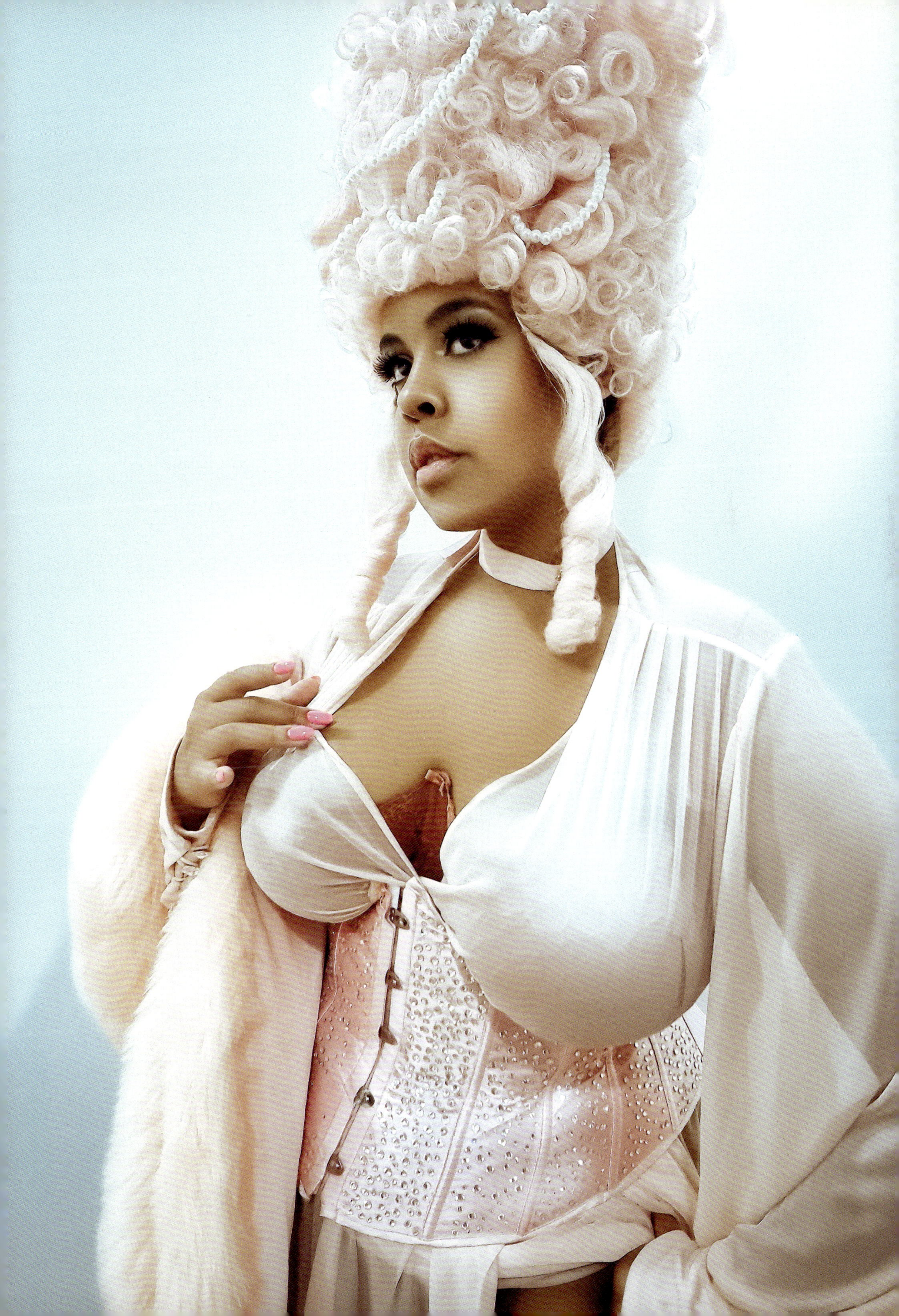

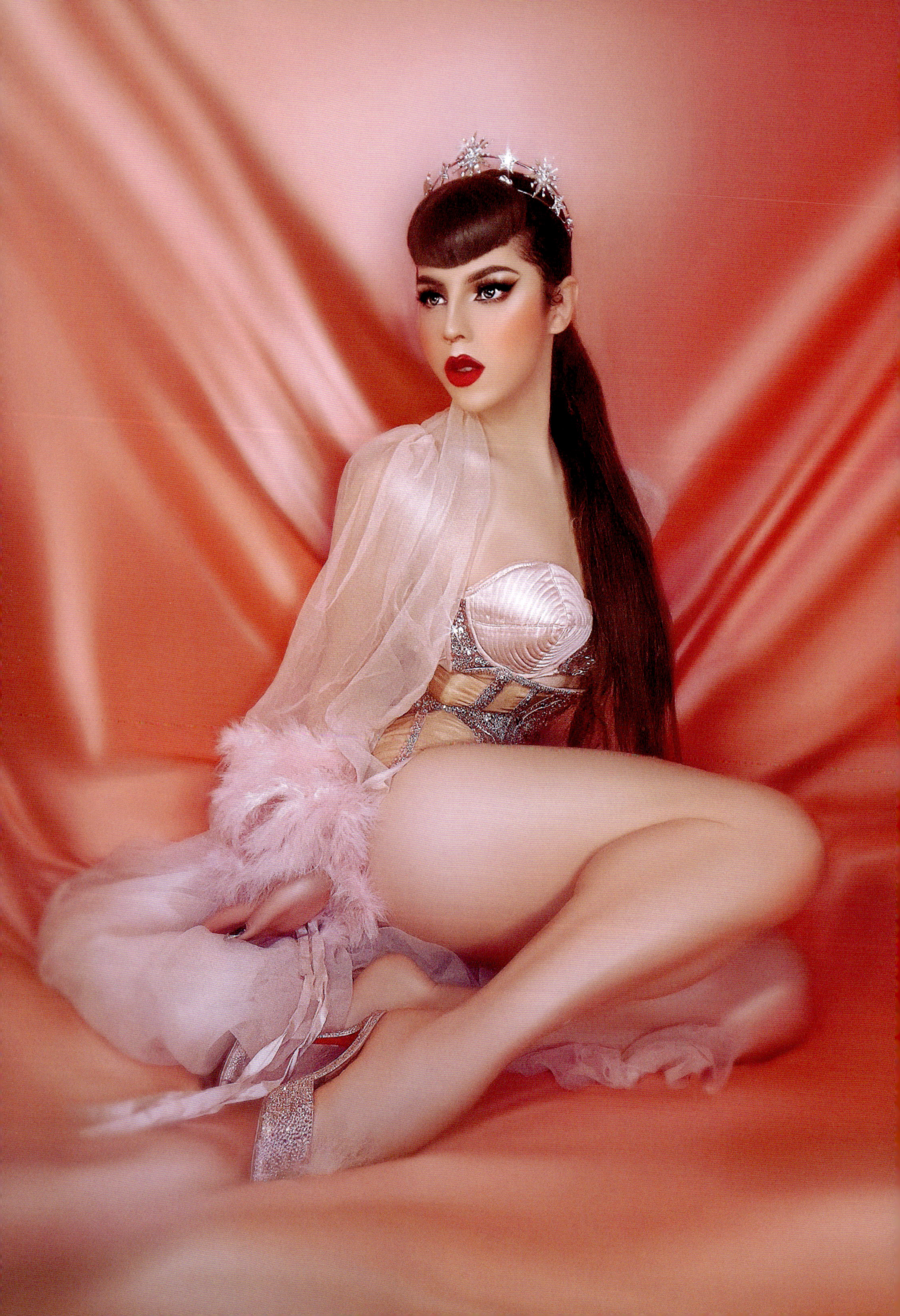

"Burlesque is a real art with a real history, and I wish people knew a little bit more about cabaret. It is for everyone. Everyone can do burlesque and cabaret, it's not just for cis women. Everyone is valid."

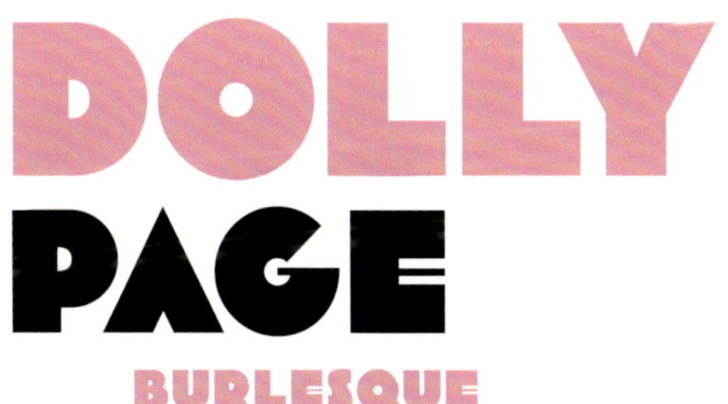

# DOLLY PAGE

## BURLESQUE

Dolly Page is a burlesque showgirl, model, and beauty influencer based in Paris. Her performances pay homage to classic pinup, luxury fashion, and Hollywood glamour, all inspirations that she mimics in the details of her aesthetic and exquisite costuming. For Dolly, performing means freedom to express herself and her art, and she loves using the stage to create fantasies for her audience.

# CLEOPANTHA

## BURLESQUE & QUEERLESQUE

"Performing brings me the utmost happiness and in addition to this, I get to meet and share stages with some of the most talented and wonderful artists from all over the globe."

Cleopantha's high-energy performances and unique style of neo-burlesque that centres her passion for dance and hip hop have gained her international renown. In recent years, she has become one of the most prominent faces in British burlesque.

At an early age, it was Cleopantha's mother who spotted her talents while on a family caravan holiday in Blackpool and decided to put her into dance lessons. Though she could only afford to send her daughter to a couple classes each week, it was enough to spark a lifelong passion for dance. Throughout her youth, Cleopantha competed in and won countless competitions, and went on to train at the Fierce Dance Academy run by international voguer Darren Pritchard, Manchester's leading performance arts college, Pendleton, and the Northern School of Contemporary Dance.

As a woman of mixed heritage coming from a working-class family in Manchester, Cleopantha is proud of her roots.

She understands that not everyone can afford to access the arts and wishes that cabaret was more accessible to working-class people. Producers often expect performers to have high-end, expensive costumes, something that caused her to miss out on several opportunities early on in her career. She wants more to be known about the true diversity of the cabaret scene, both in terms of the types of performance it encompasses and the types of people that perform within it.

Cleopantha was born to perform and through cabaret is able to share her passion with audiences all over the world.

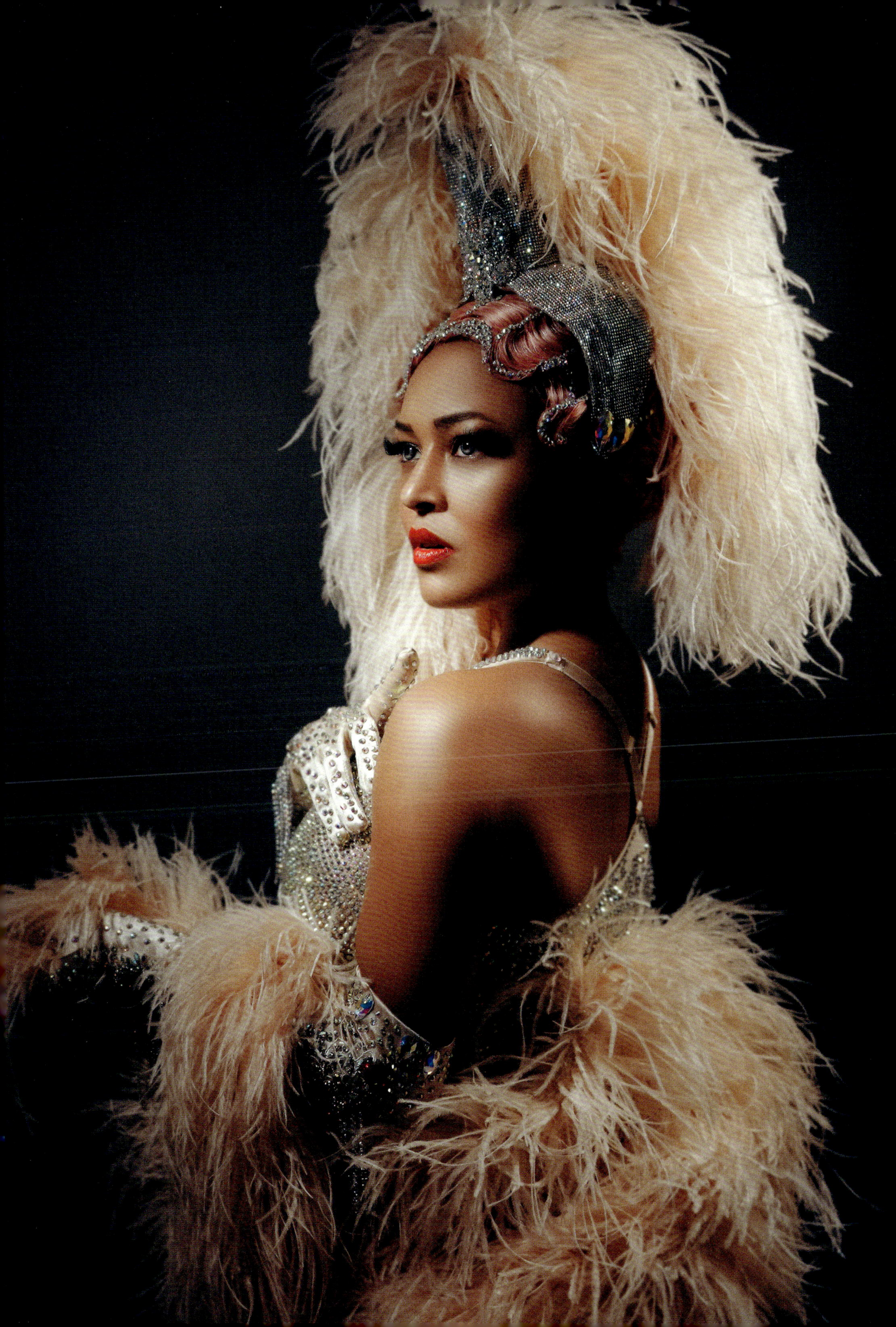

"I got to a point in my life where I was desperately trying to love myself. Performing with The Cocoa Butter Club allowed me to dive deeper into who I truly was, and so the loving began."

# RUDY
# JEEVANJEE

## QUEERLESQUE & DRAGLESQUE

Rudy Jeevanjee is all about royalty, the embodiment of a deity that taps into a divine experience of where masculine and feminine energies meet. Rudy is always serving full-bodied non-binary finery, with performances that evoke a spirit of freedom, sensuality, and power.

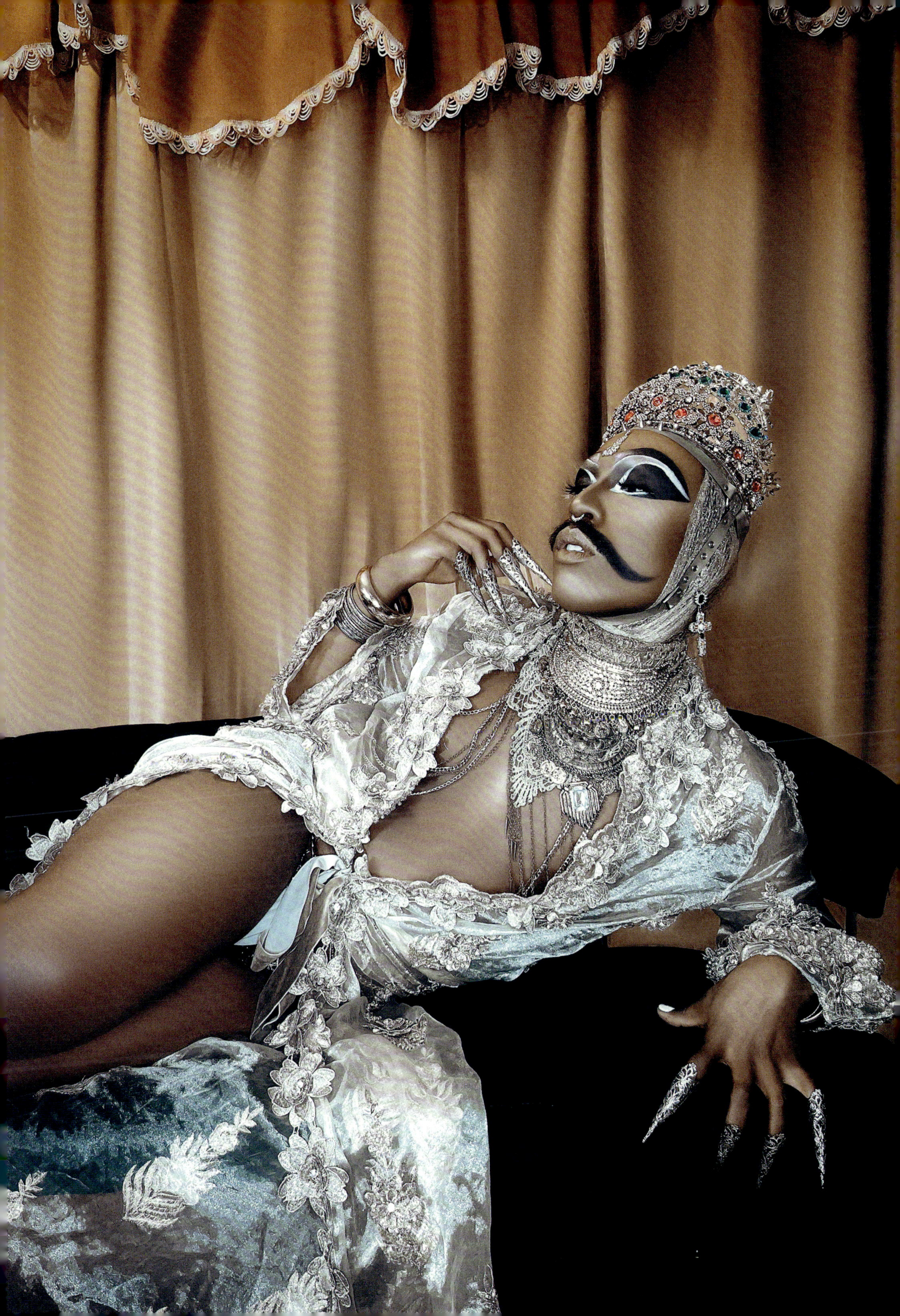

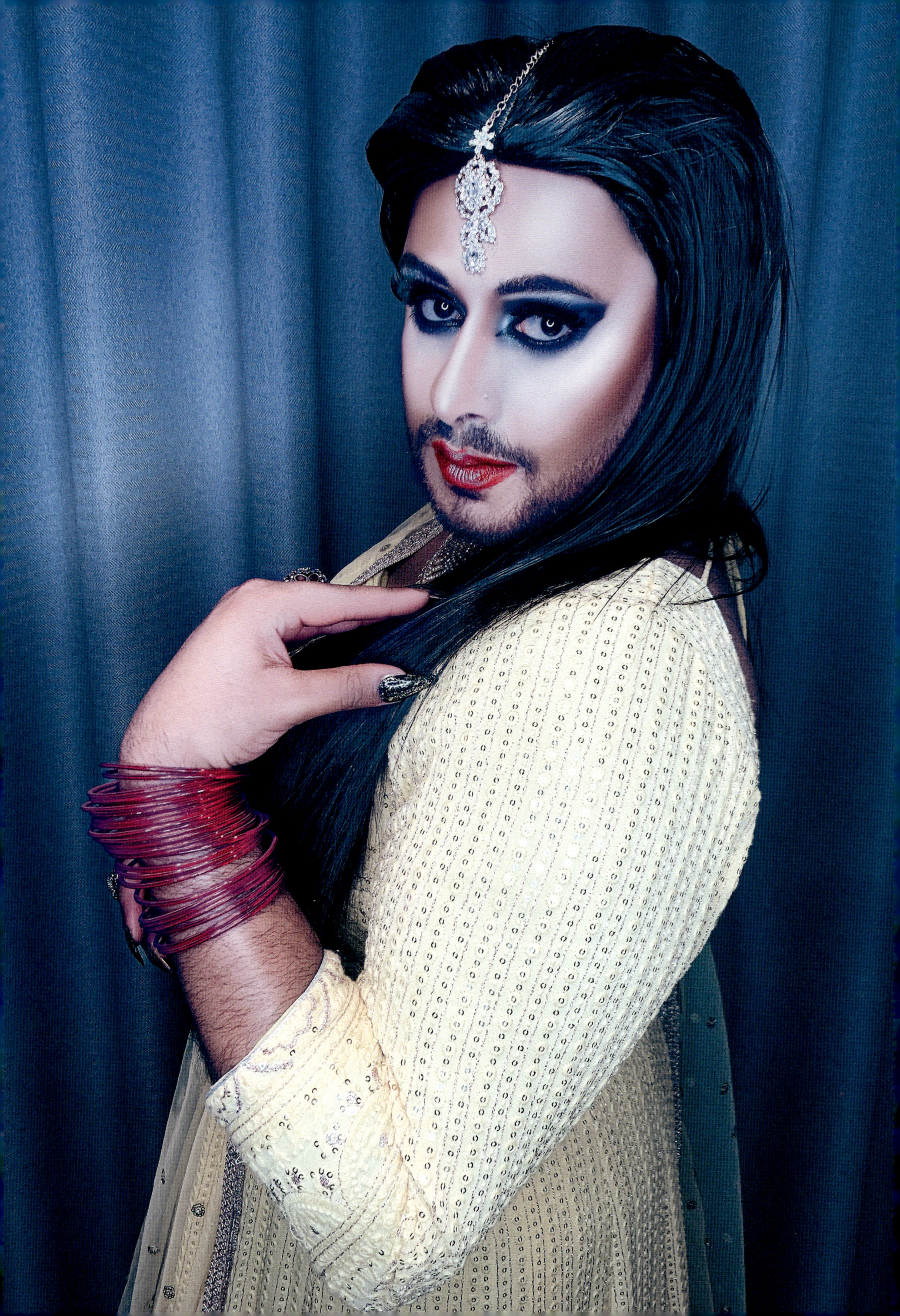

# LADY BUSHRA

## DRAG QUEEN

Lady Bushra is the brainchild of British Asian comedian Amir, originally
from Bradford. Shortlisted for the 2021 BBC New Comedy Awards, Lady
Bushra performs her show Drag Comedy Cabaret across the UK. Known for
her lip-syncs, stand-up, and one-liners, her comedy is witty, satirical, and
often scurrilous, combining South Asian sensibilities with British humour in
a way that challenges stereotypes and pushes audiences to a sweet spot of
discomfort and hilarity.

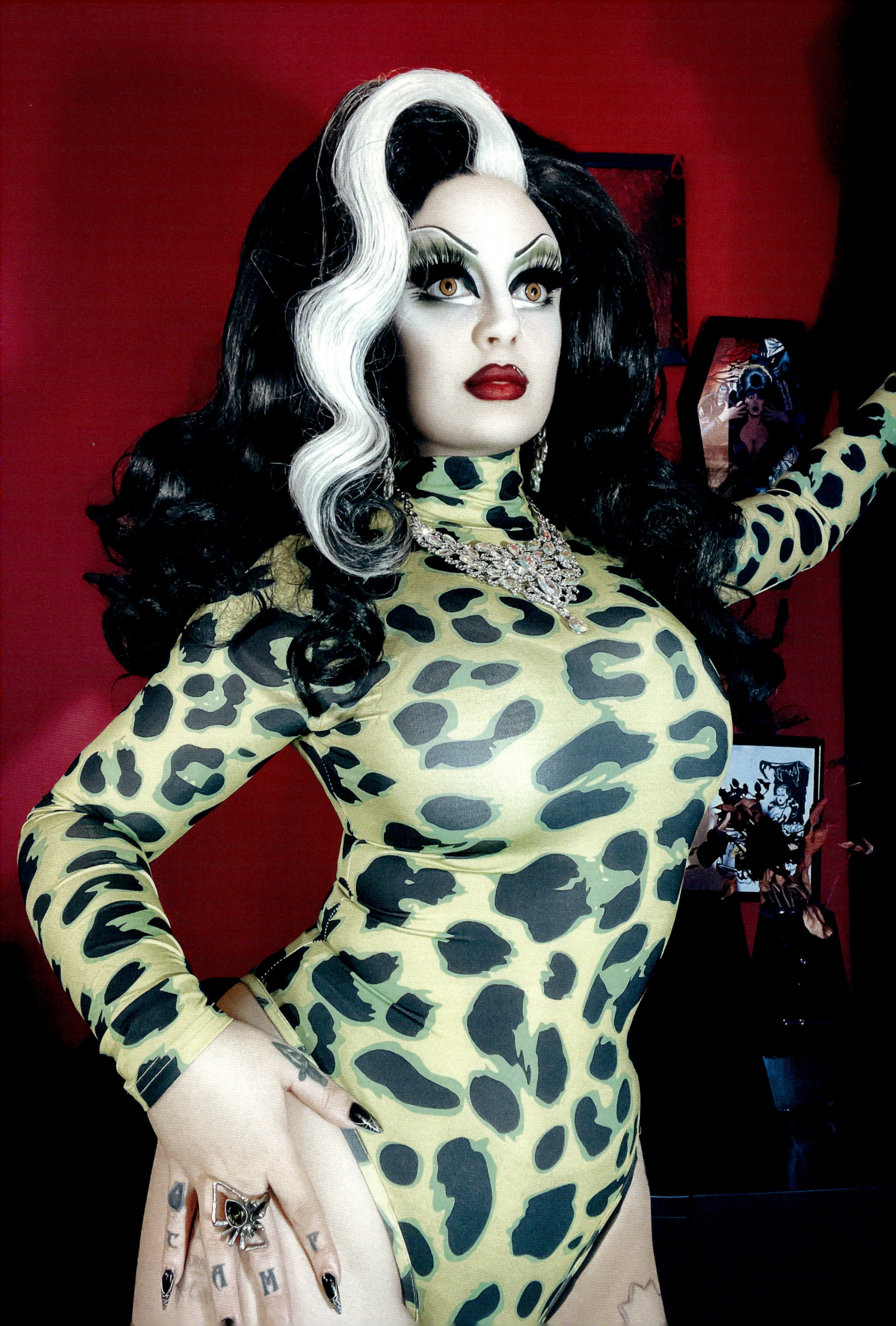

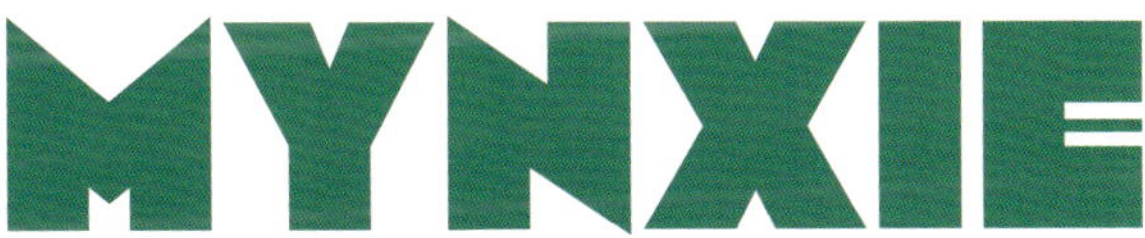

## DRAG QUEEN

Mynxie is a vampy, hyper-feminine Drag Queen who's been hosting, singing, stripping, and DJing on the London queer scene for the better part of a decade. She's inspired by campy horror aesthetics, exaggerated femininity, and kitsch retro glamour.

"My dream would be the return of cabaret clubs and music halls. We make people feel things in the moment that can bring joy for a second or prompt lasting change."

# CAROUSEL HART

## QUEERLESQUE

Carousel Hart loves to create cabaret acts based on people from the past who lived on the edges of society, from 1960s strip clubs to Victorian circus sideshows. Carousel's looks are big, bright, and colourful, born from the freedom of coming out and reflecting the joyful feeling of no longer being in the closet.

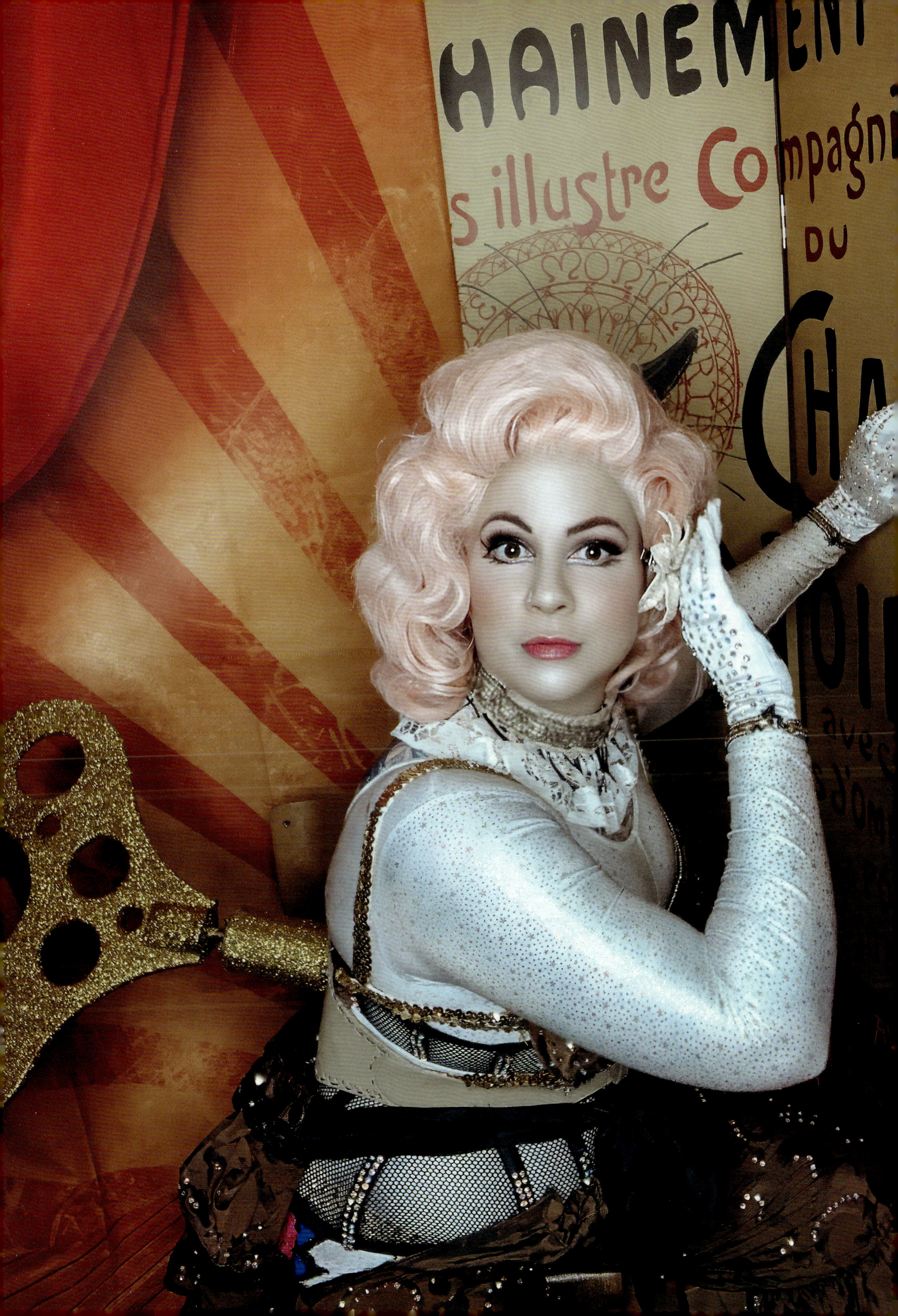
HAINEMENT
s illustre Compagni
DU
CHA
avec

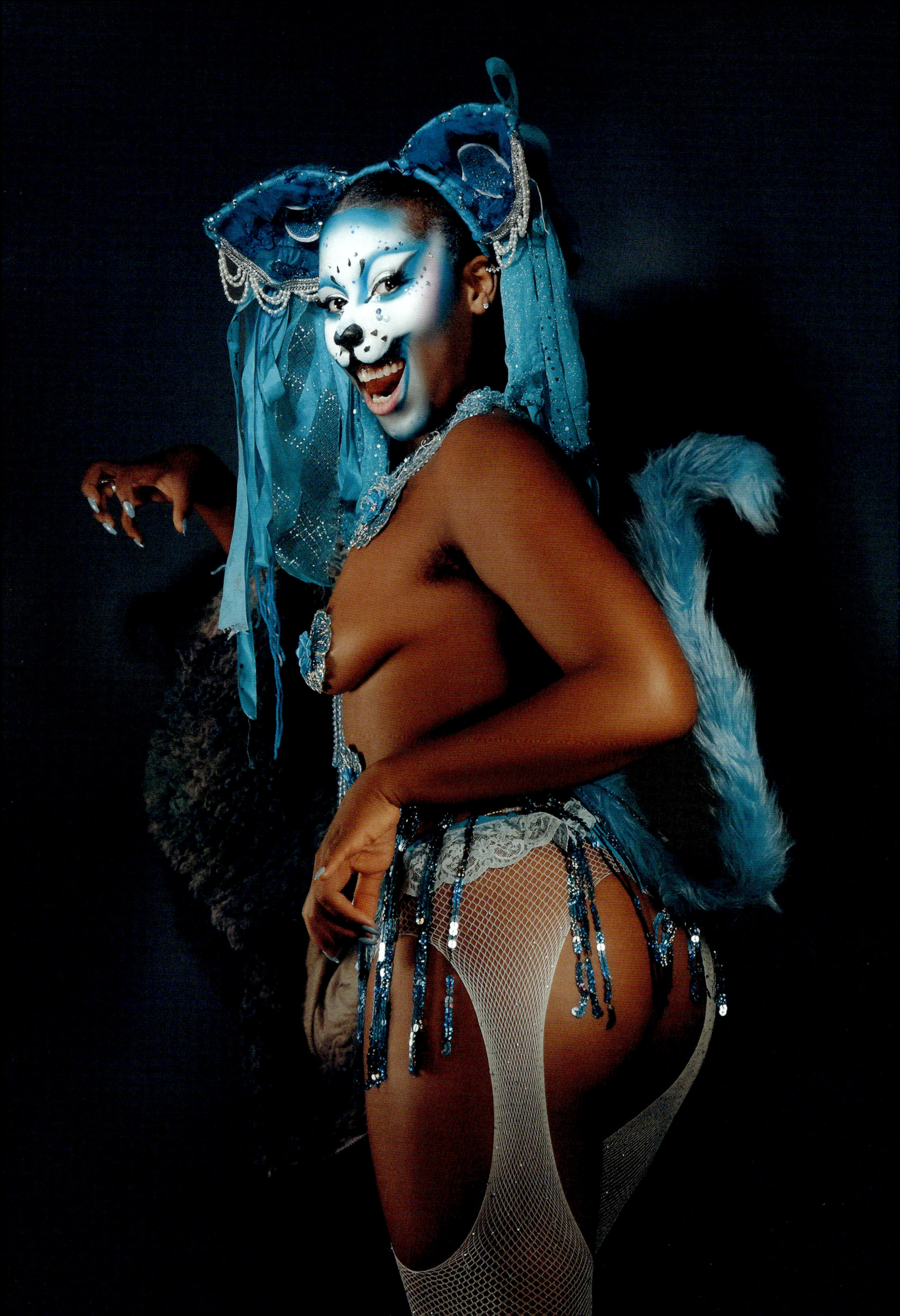

# PORSCHA PRESENT

## DRAG THING

Porscha Present is a trans, non-binary, Afro-Caribbean Drag Thing/King, extraordinary musician, and performance artist. In their performances, they play with song, dance, lip-sync, and storytelling as well as a kinky love for food and mess on stage. Their costumes are bright, colourful, campy, and often clownish.

# MOLLY BETH MOROSSA
## DRAG THING & QUEERLESQUE

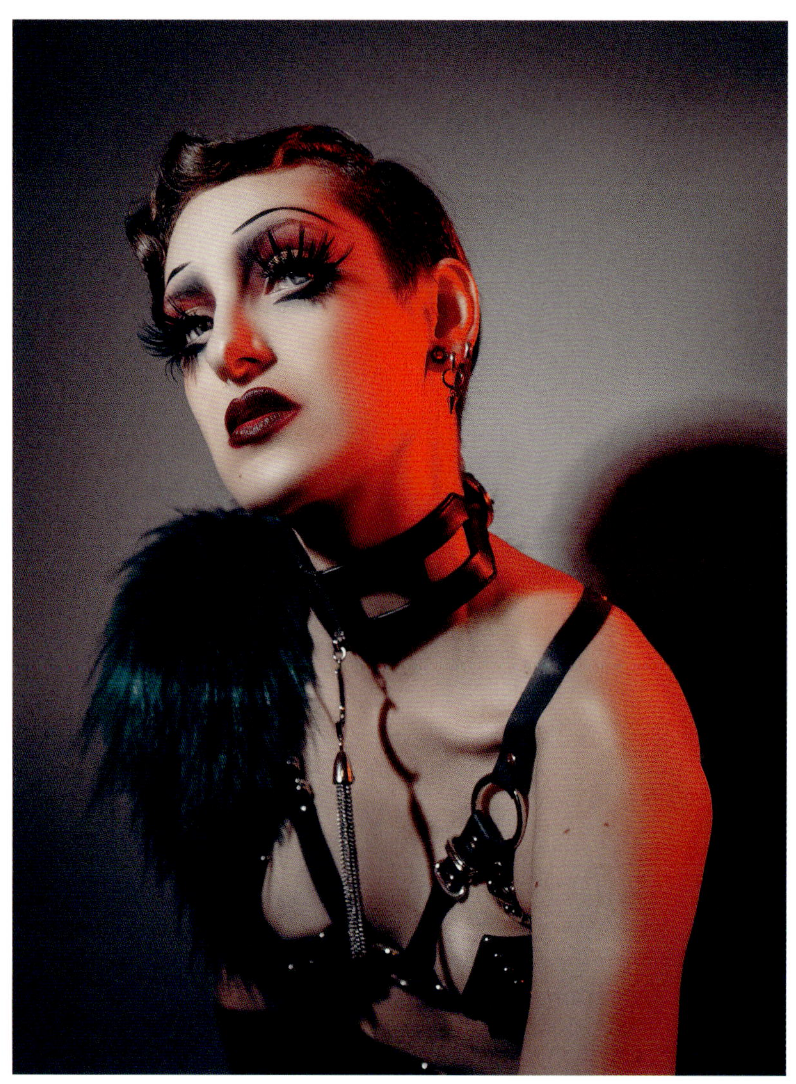

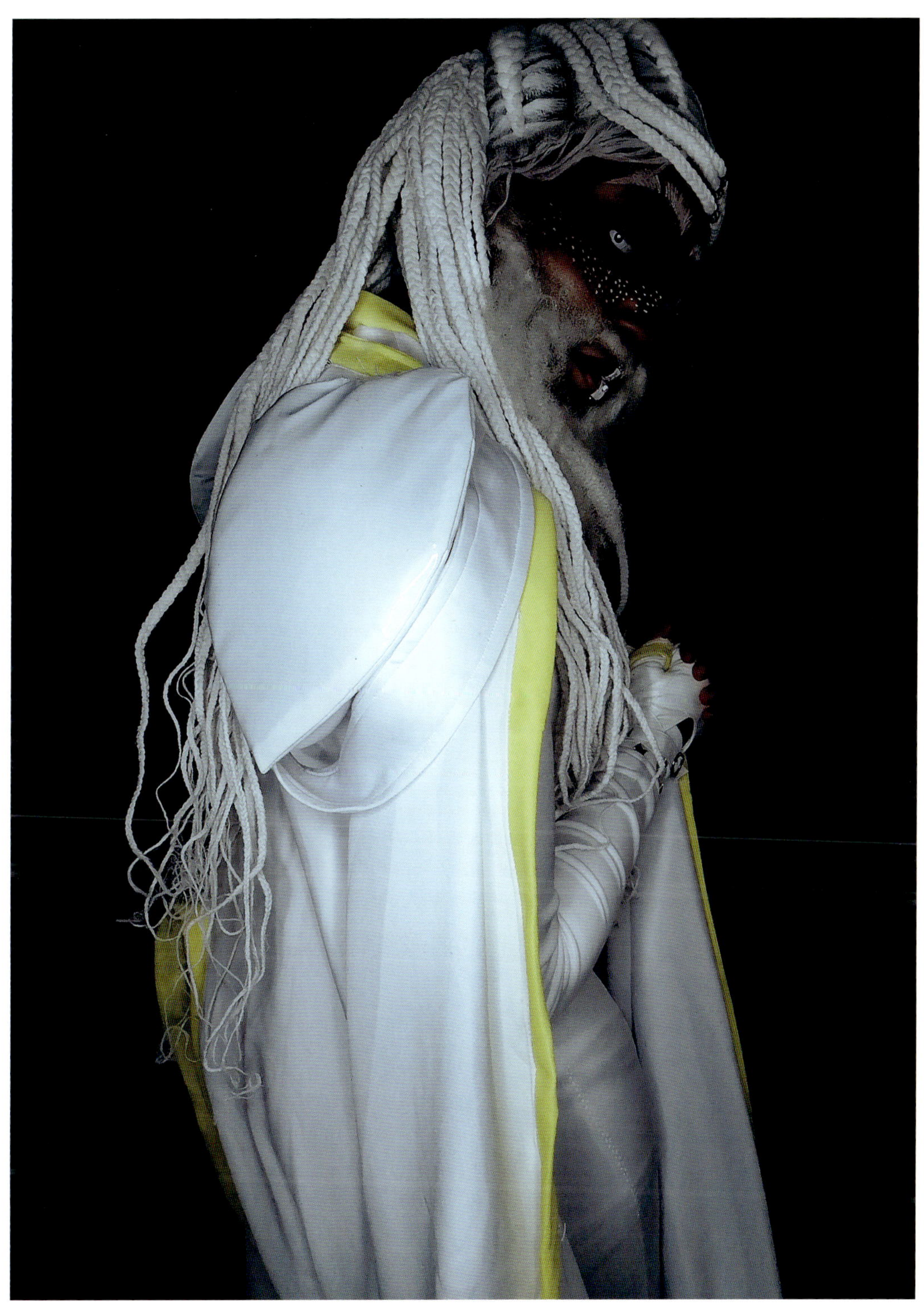

# MANLY MANNINGTON

**DRAG KING**

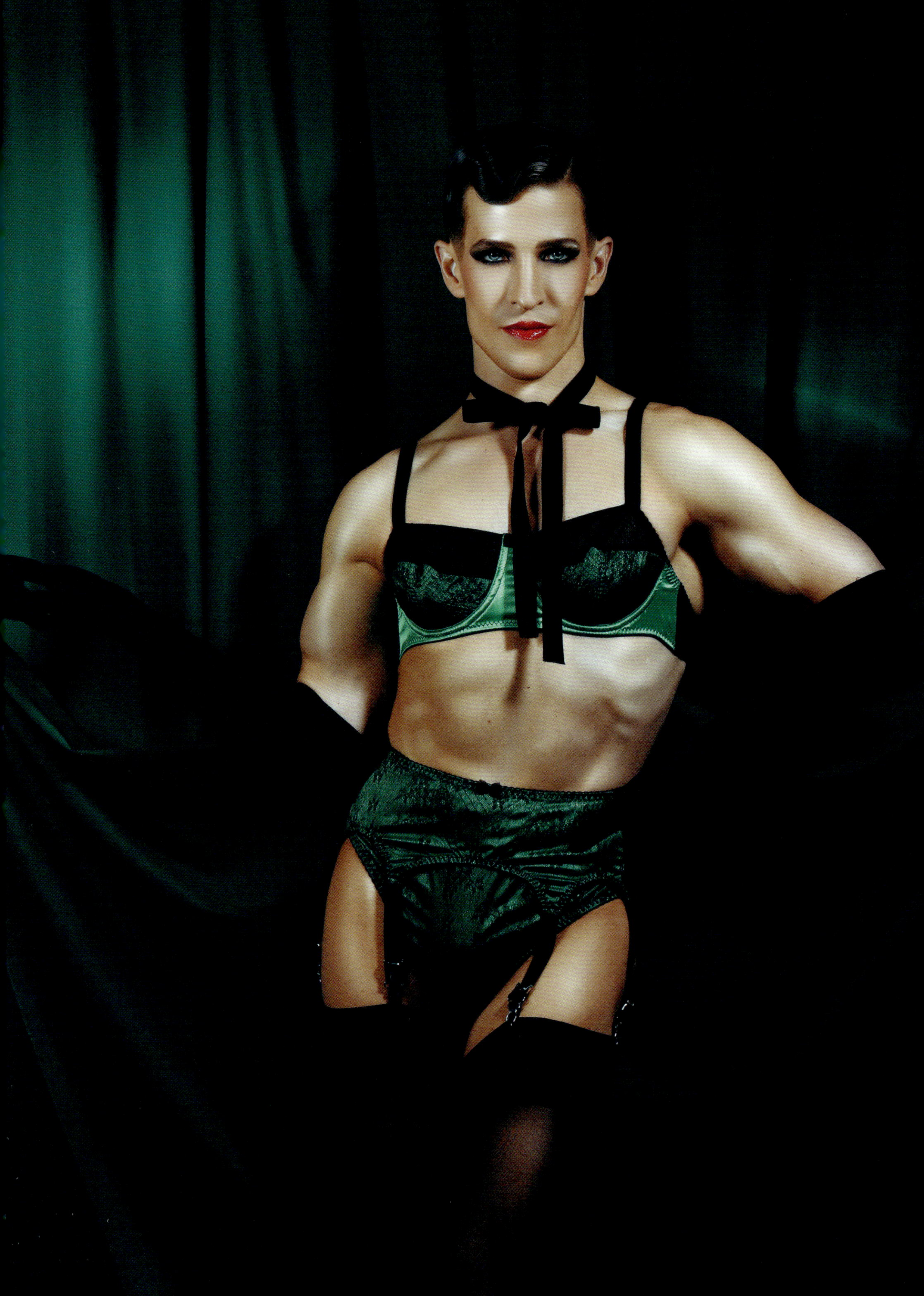

"I feel like a superhero (or supervillain!) whenever I'm on stage. I don't have to think. My body takes over and I feel like I just get to be free."

# JAKE DUPREE

## BURLESQUE

Jake DuPree is a non-binary burlesque performer known for polish, grace, and finesse. They come with an impressive pedigree—their debut performance was with none other than Dita Von Teese. Alongside burlesque, Jake is a professional dancer with stage and screen credits, a top LA barre instructor, and an influential lingerie model.

# MX CYANIDE

## QUEERLESQUE & DRAGLESQUE

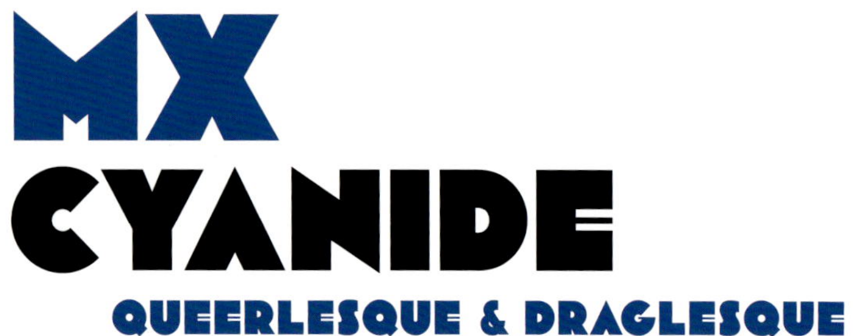

Mx Cyanide is a proud transgender performer who rose from the filth and glamour of Soho's underground burlesque scene to twist the sexual with the perverse, political, and painful for audiences across the world. They live to subvert what sensual burlesque is and push it towards what it can be, giving the audience space to leave all preconceptions at the door.

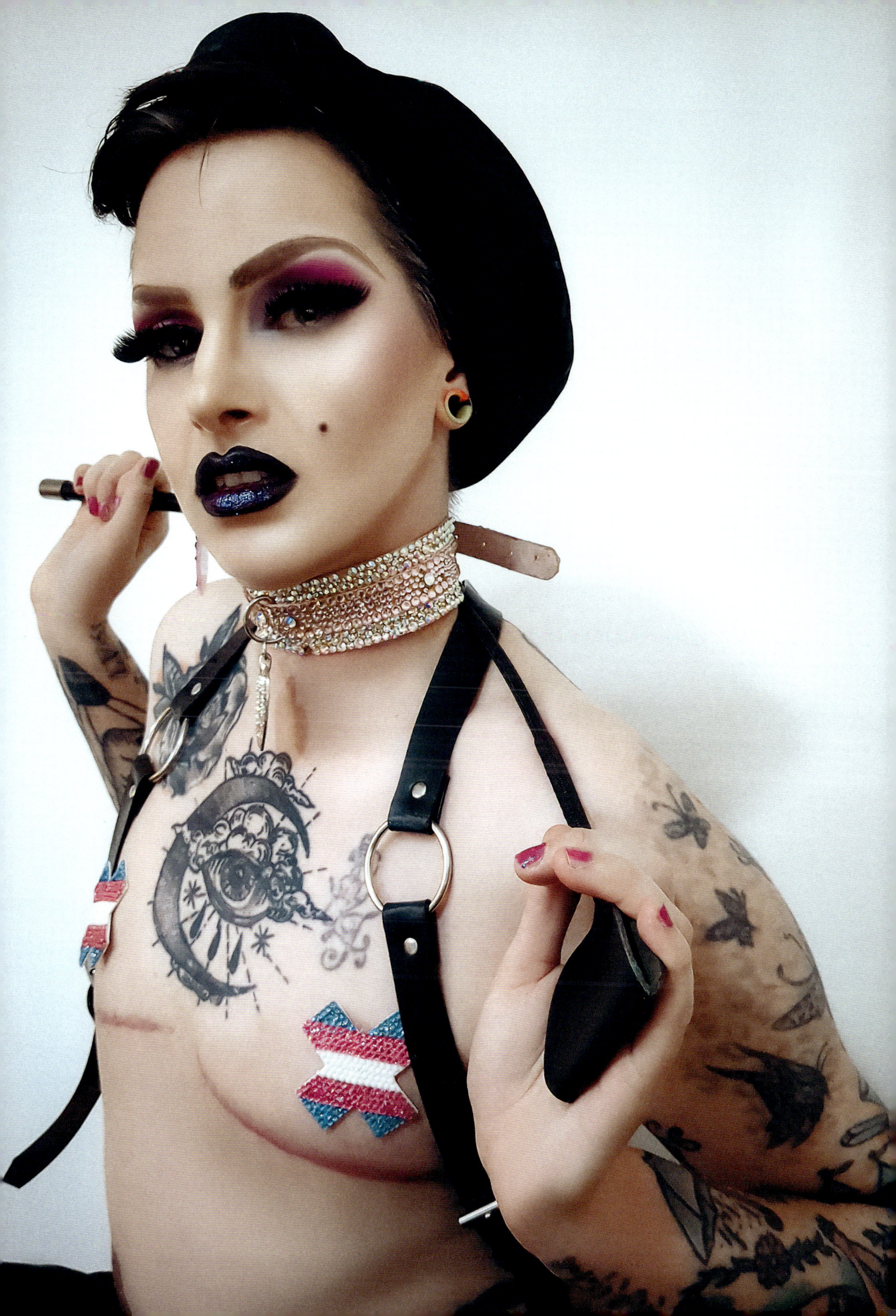

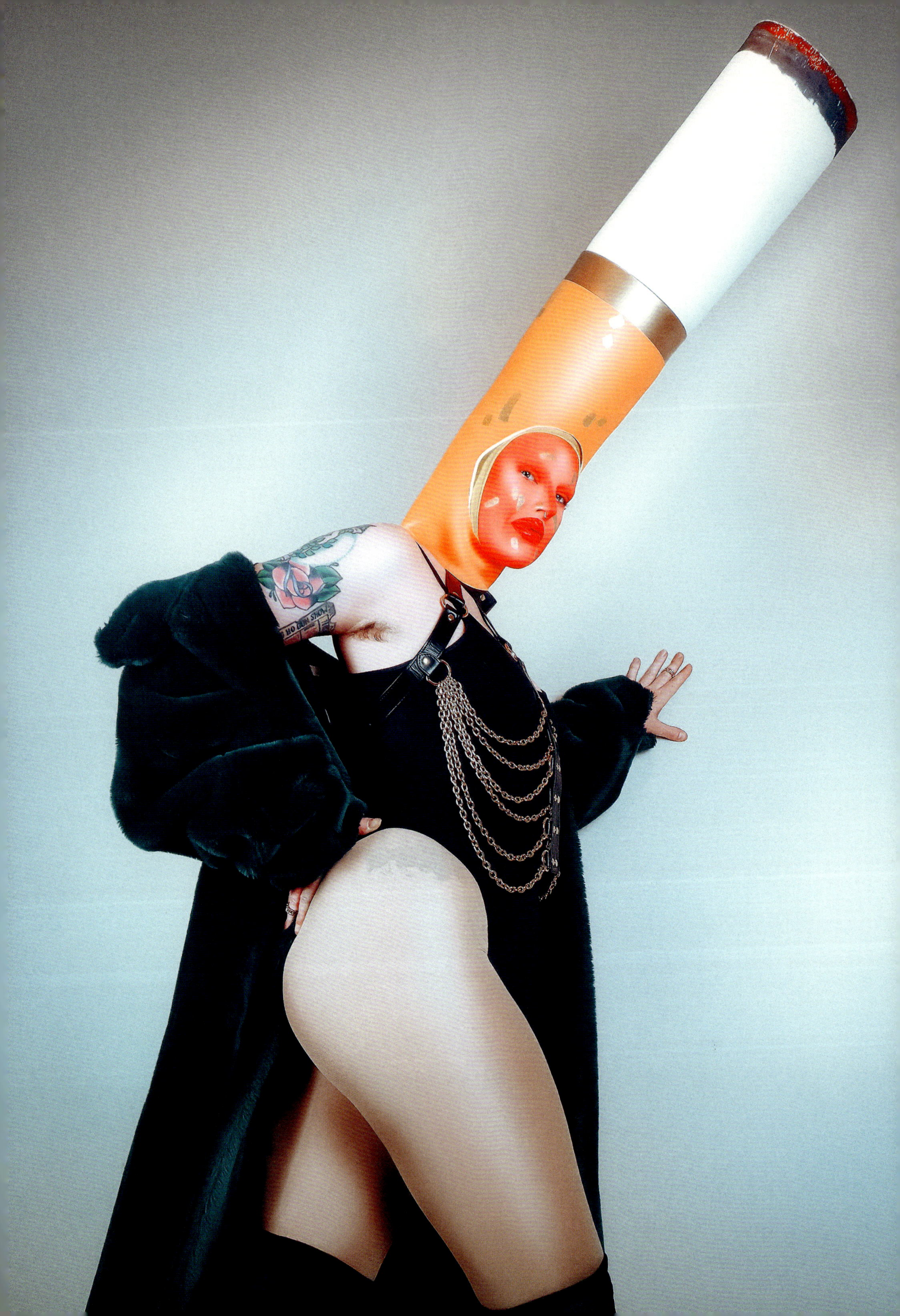

# BIPOLAR ABDUL

## NON-BINARY DRAG

Bipolar Abdul is a non-binary drag artist from Doncaster, Yorkshire, who is bursting with pop culture references, satirical commentary on society, and general irreverence. True to their working class background, their performances and aesthetics have a gritty, DIY feel, presented in an editorial, fashion-forward way.

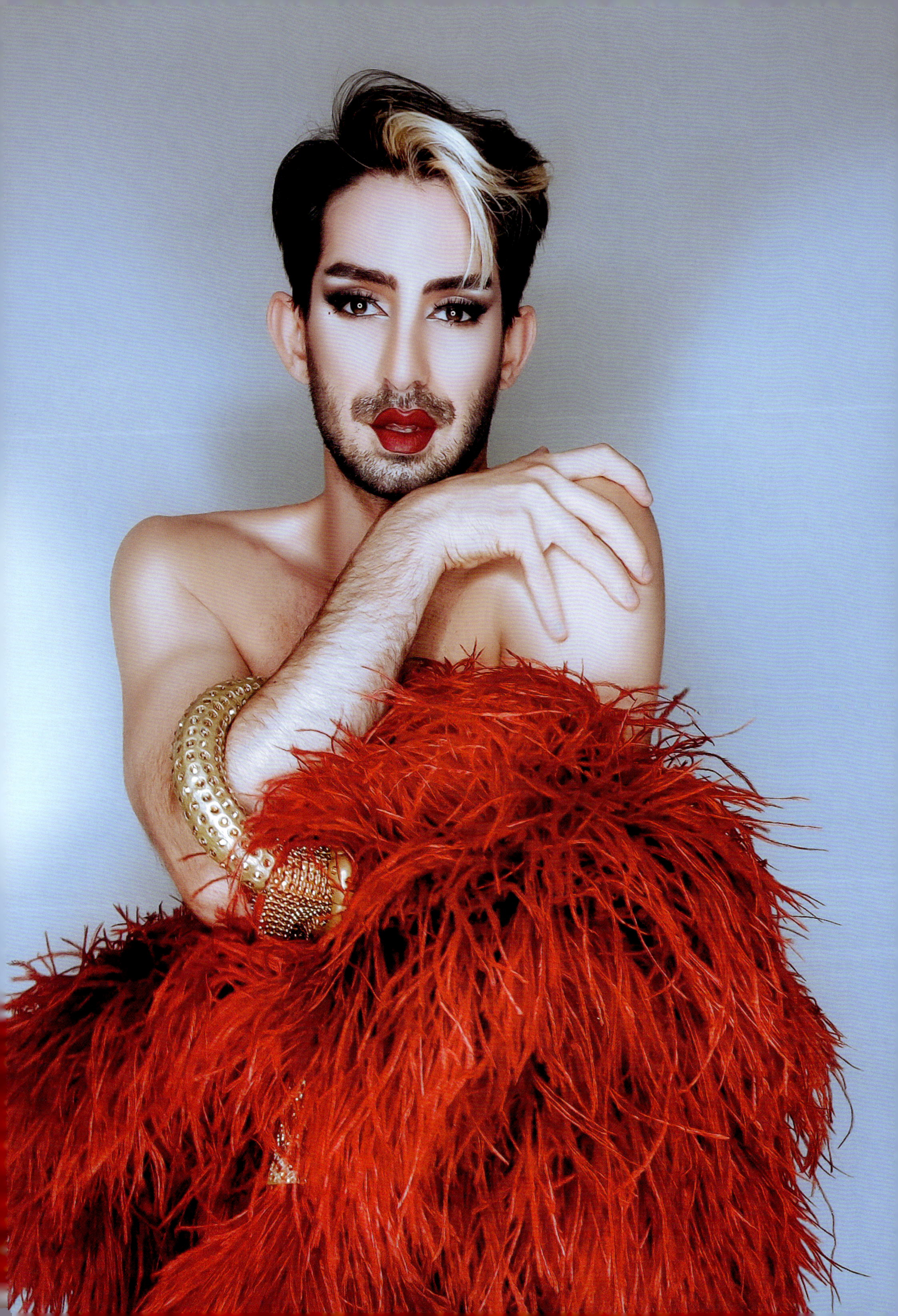

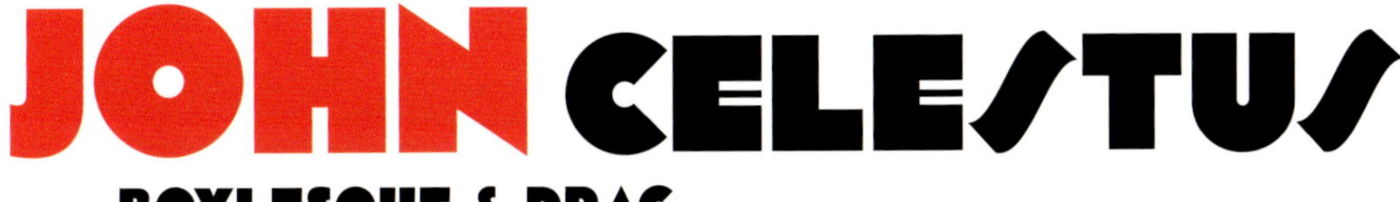

# JOHN CELESTUS
## BOYLESQUE & DRAG

> **"Artists are drops in the rain that will change the world, and it's a privilege to be part of this rain."**

John Celestus can admit that when he started performing in 2010, his motivations for joining the cabaret scene were selfish and self-indulgent, but soon they became about the audience and the power to make change. As a boylesque performer, compère, circus artist, and professional mermaid, John Celestus, like many other cabaret performers, finds performing to be both a mode of self-expression and an outlet that encourages open dialogue surrounding sexuality, liberation, and freedom.

He is a firm believer that performers can change the world and his personal duty is to create unique experiences for his audiences. John also uses his time on stage to help challenge the audience's views on gender and social norms. From his elaborate outfits, dramatic makeup, and overall androgynous imagery, he pushes the audience to question their beliefs and examine a different way of existing outside of the standard norms. Perhaps expressing himself as authentically as possible will inspire someone else to become more comfortable with their true self.

Beyond the stage and behind the lights, there is much hard work that goes into creating this kind of art, especially as someone who uses their body as an instrument, and John hopes that one day people will see and understand the complexity of it all. He also hopes for the industry itself, that everyone can begin to work with and not against each other. He hopes one day the industry will reflect genuine diversity.

# COCO DEVILLE

## QUEERLESQUE & BURLESQUE

Coco Deville is an award-winning, international cabaret chameleon with over two decades of professional stage experience. Armed with a degree in contemporary theatre and choreography, the spotlight is her playground. From 1960s gogo gal to fierce femme fatale, her trademark twist on burlesque fuses body positivity, dance, skillful audience interaction, and a flamboyant and infectious stage presence.

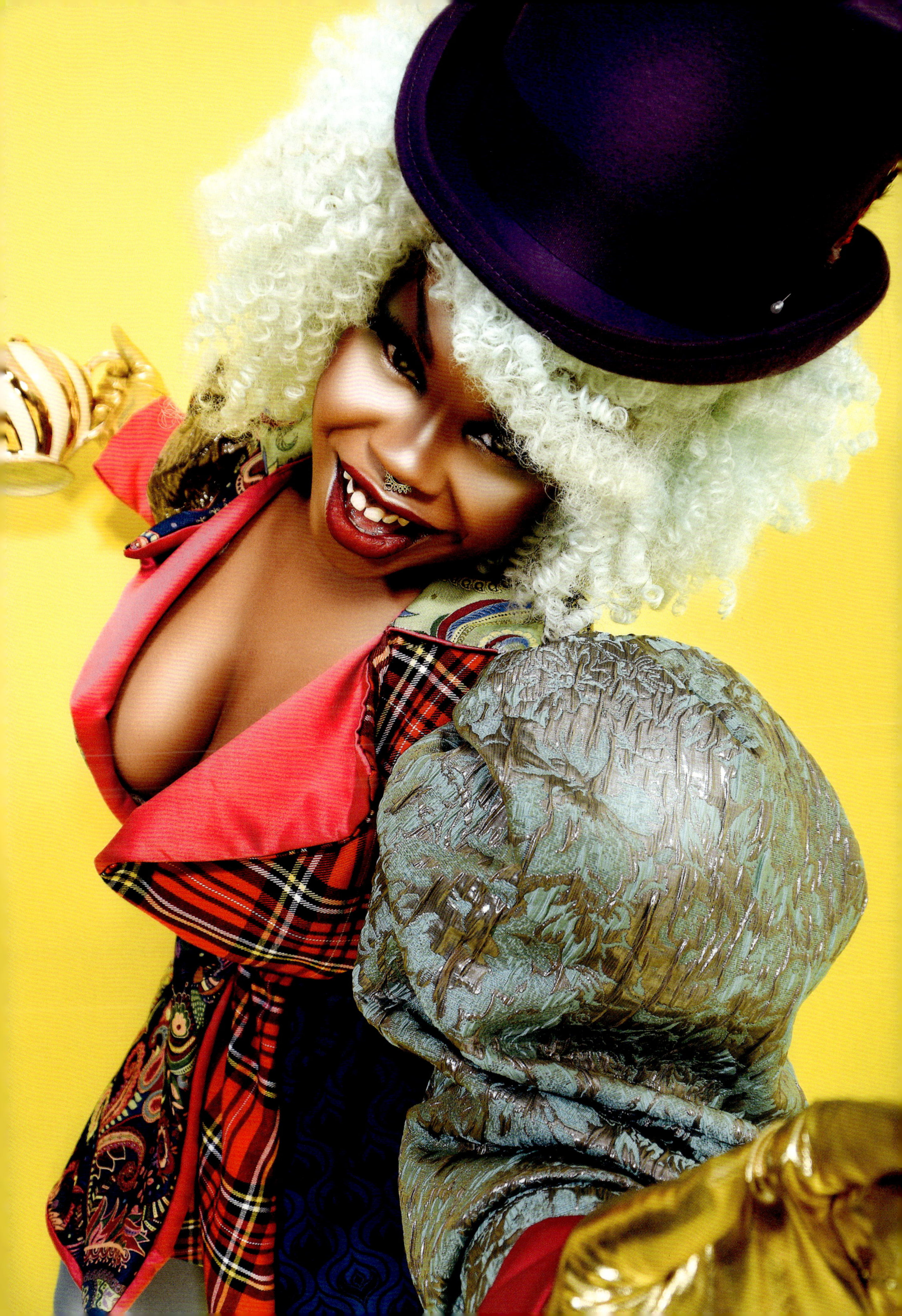

# PI
## THE MIME
### QUEERLESQUE

Pi is a mime. Or a clown. Or both! Drawing inspiration from training in traditional mime and clowning, Pi creates work that explores the clown/mime from a modern and queer perspective. Think Chaplin, Pierrot, Marceau, and Harlequin, but through a gender-bending pop-culture lens. Too modern for the old-school circus and too queer for the commercial theatre stage, Pi found a home in cabaret.

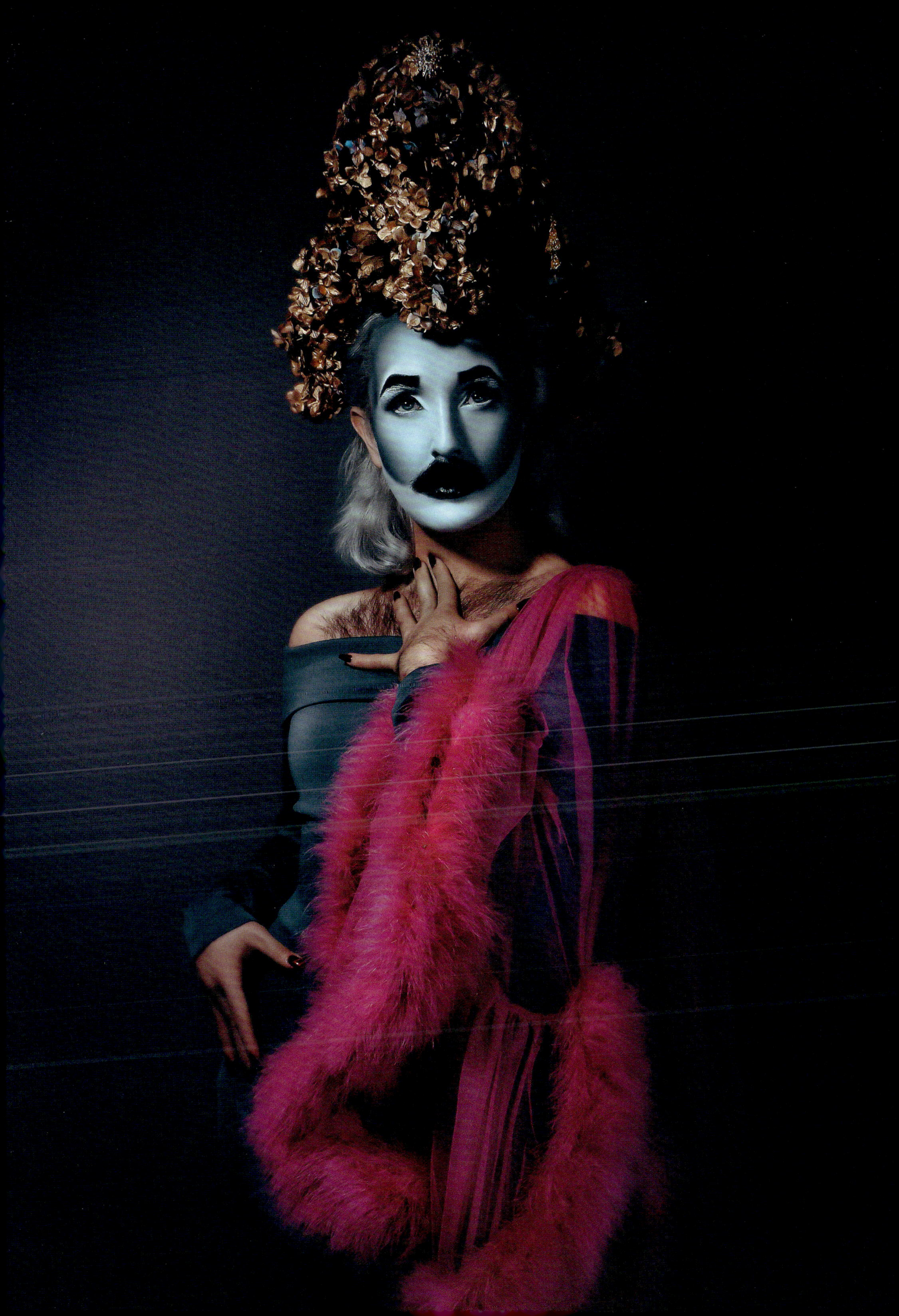

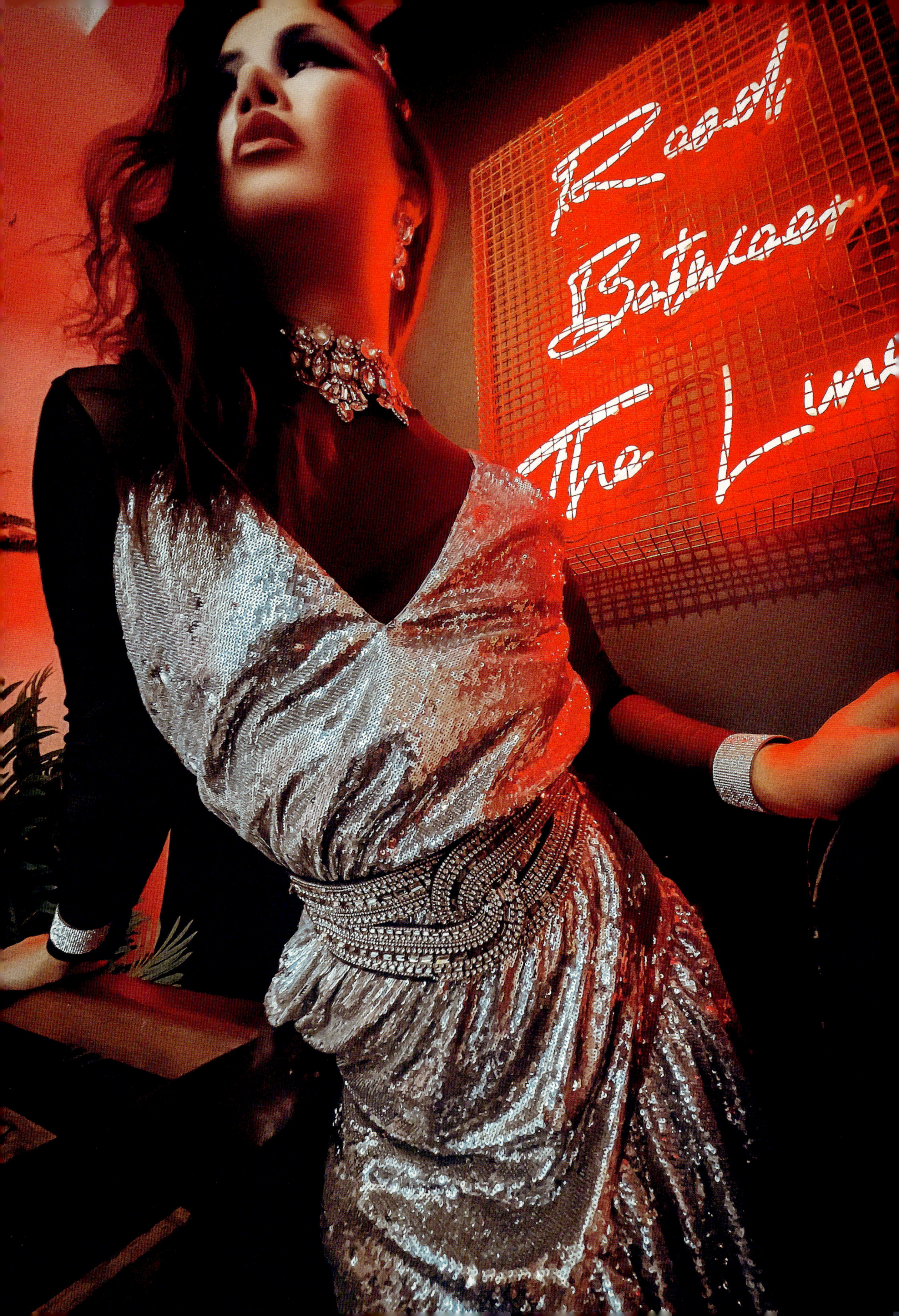
Read
Between
The Line

Versace meets the Matrix, meets Mortal Kombat, meets the Spice Girls, Jvst Tina is a Drag Queen who was born in the fashion industry, and on stage, embodies the fierce femininity of musical icons. She often builds her aesthetic on archive pieces she has collected while working for major designers,

"We need to be willing to learn from each other so that we can improve this community that can be very accepting, inspiring, life-changing, and supportive."

# LADY BLUE
# PHOENIX
## BURLESQUE & QUEERLESQUE

Lady Blue Phoenix is a neo-burlesque, plus size, gender fluid, bisexual, disabled burlesque performer, and an award-winning member of the Foxes Troupe. A force of nature, charisma, and confidence, their acts range from political to classical, aiming to change opinions of what burlesque is and can be.

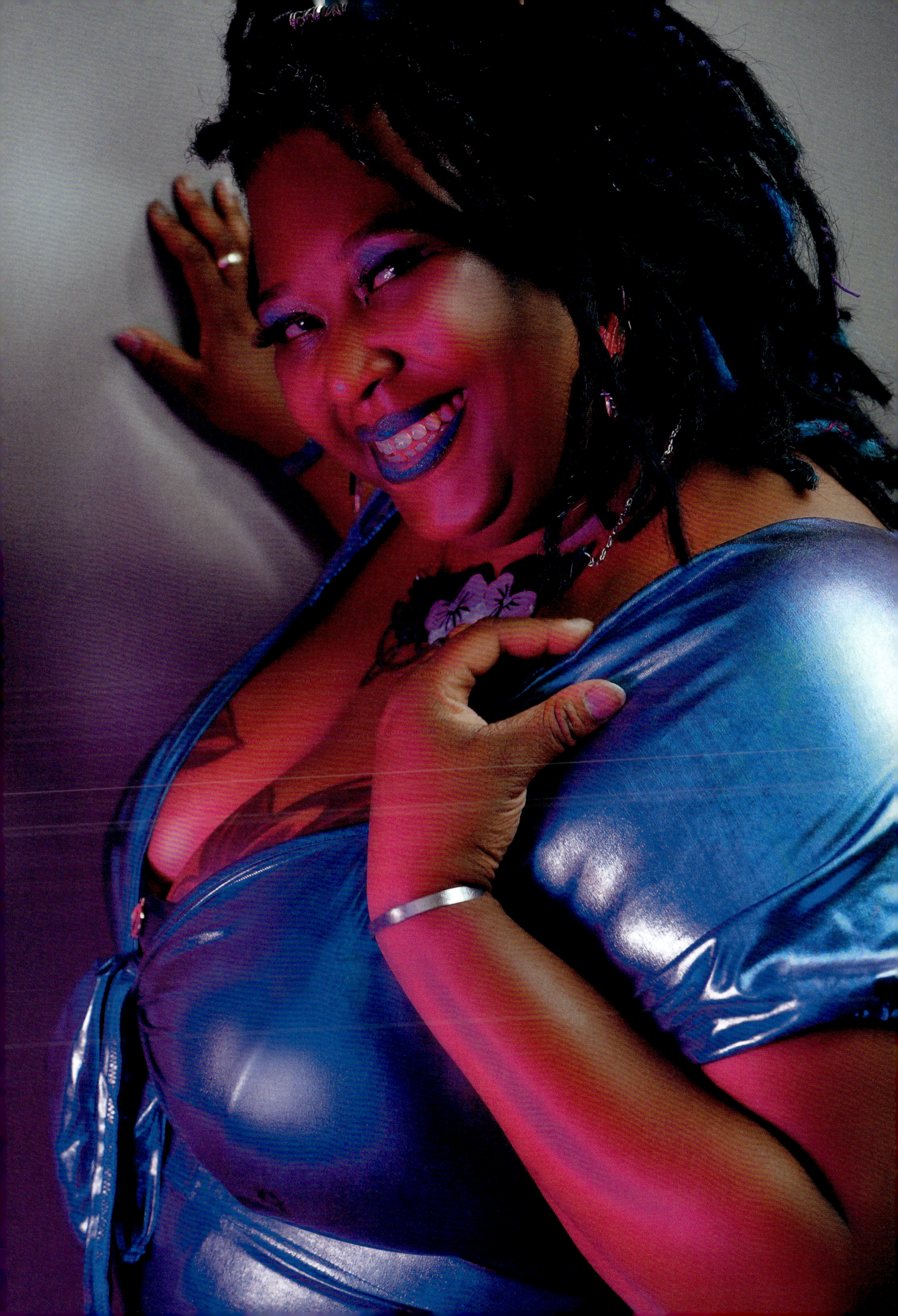

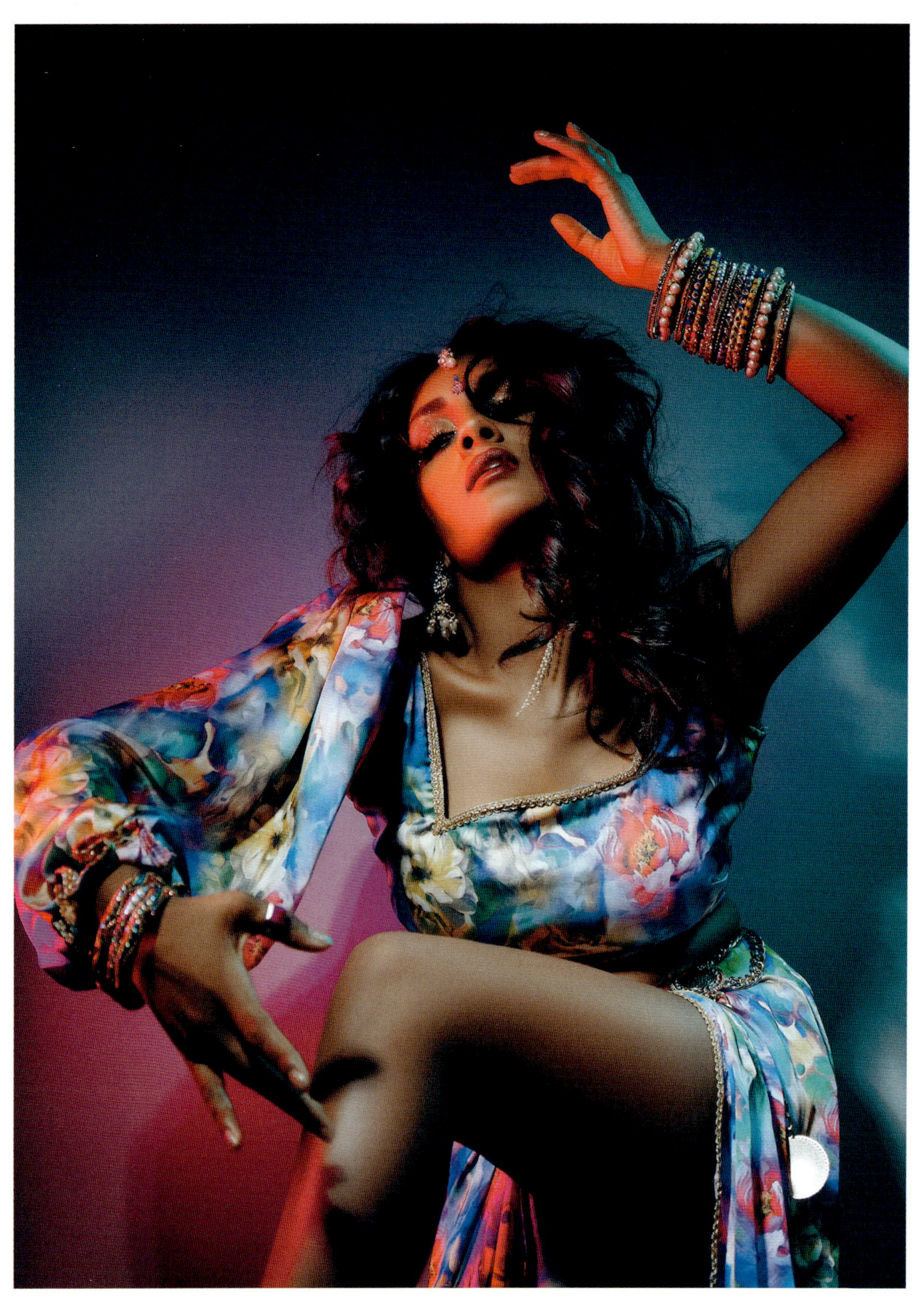

# KAAJEL

## BOLLYWOOD CABARET & QUEERLESQUE

# DEEVA D
## BURLESQUE & BEARLESQUE

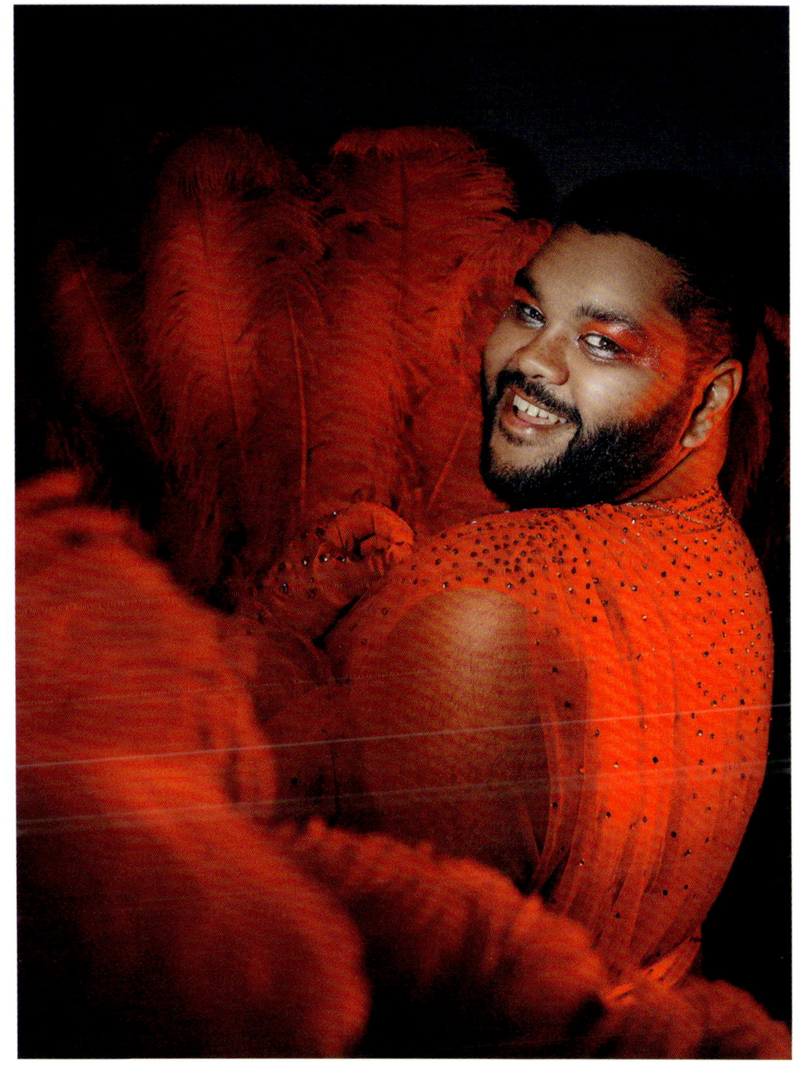

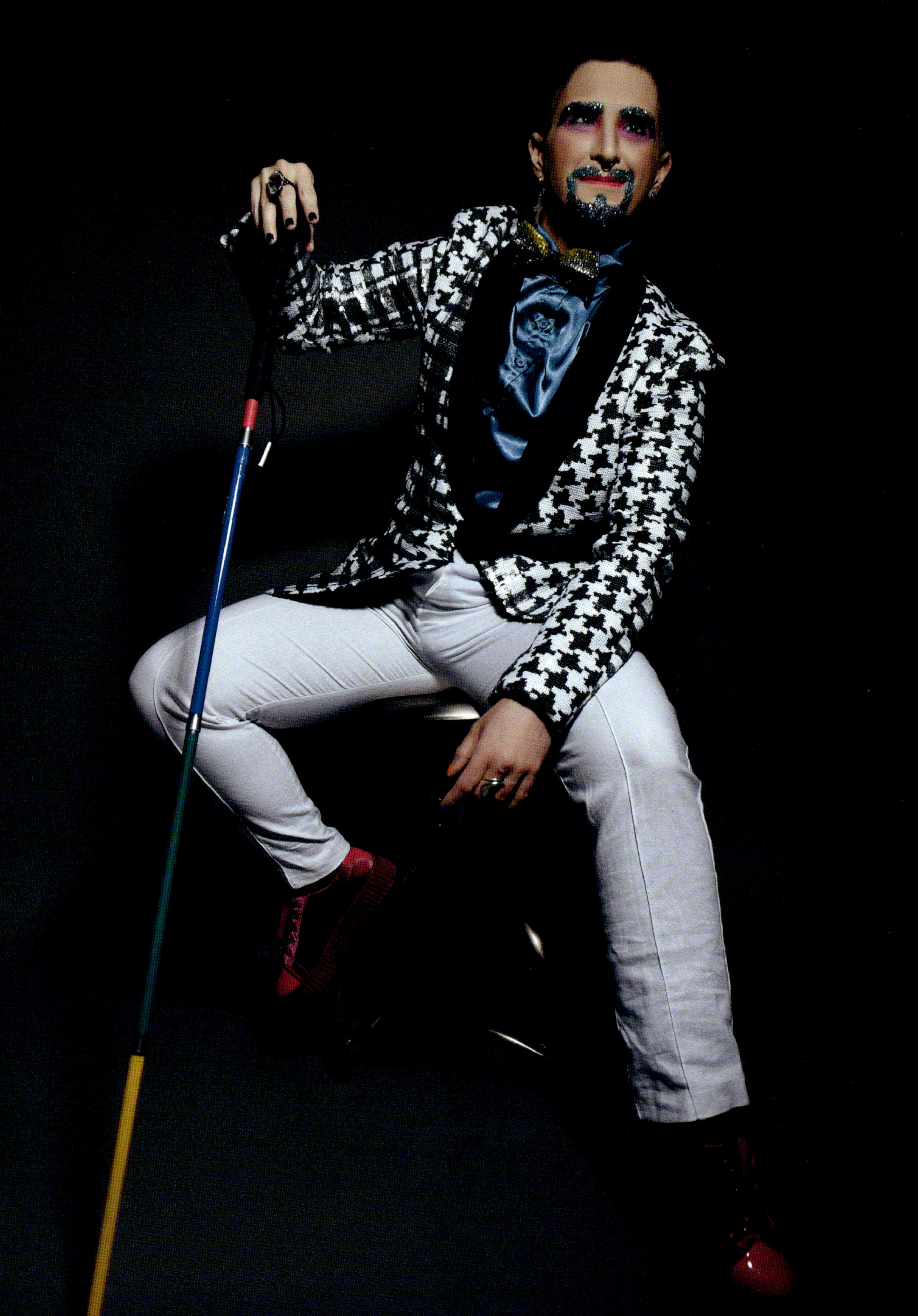

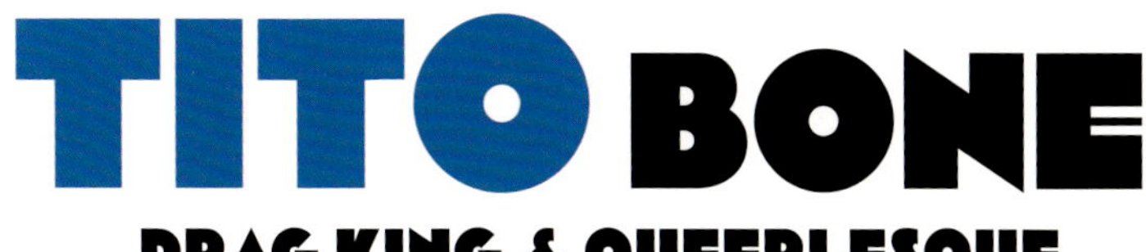

# TITO BONE
## DRAG KING & QUEERLESQUE

"Access is more than ramps and braille signs. It is how spaces are designed, how shows are run, and sometimes even just what we expect of each other."

As a blind Drag King, circus, sideshow, and queerlesque performer, Tito Bone chooses to control the narrative. From their Drag King parody of "I Will Always Love You," dedicated to their cane, to audio-described stripteases, Tito adds a touch of humour and lightness when discussing their lived experience as a queer disabled person and uses their voice and body to create unique and entertaining performances.

Performing on their own terms is necessary and empowering, and every moment Tito is on stage they are bringing more visibility to queer disabled people that are often left out of the equation. Tito believes there is still a long way to go when it comes to accessibility in the cabaret industry and queer community. It isn't enough to just have disabled performers in a show if the spaces are not safe for them—and even then, providing an accessible space goes deeper than physical adjustments to a venue.

Tito's advocacy for themselves and their community stretches far beyond the stage. Their company Quiplash, created with their wxfe Al, aims to develop those safe spaces and demand more accessibility, both in the cabaret scene and the wider environment. Tito's work shows that these spaces are sorely needed— their cabaret show at Sophiensaele in Berlin, *Unsightly Drag and Friends*, that included 12 queer disabled artists, sold out a week of shows and workshops.

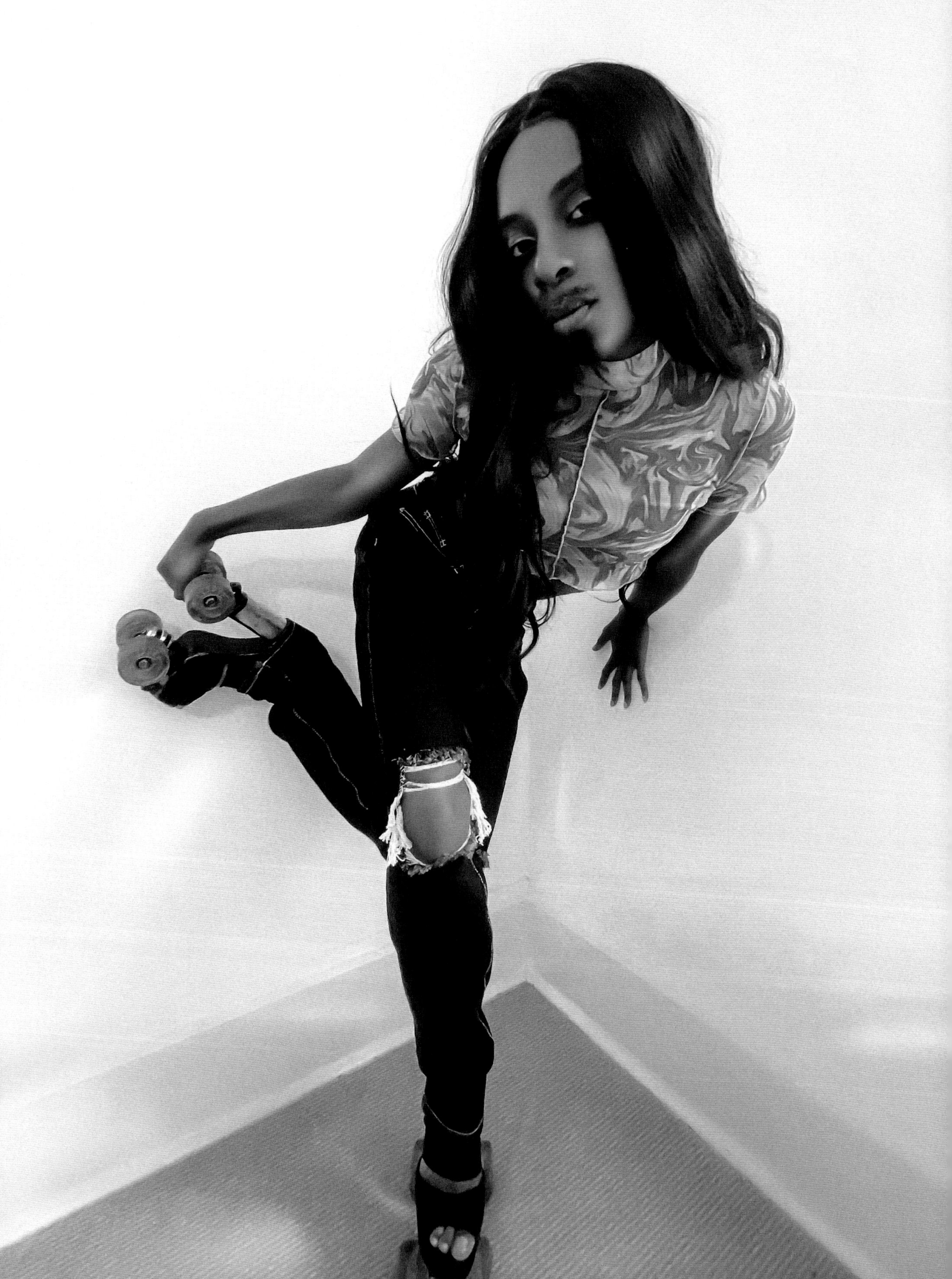

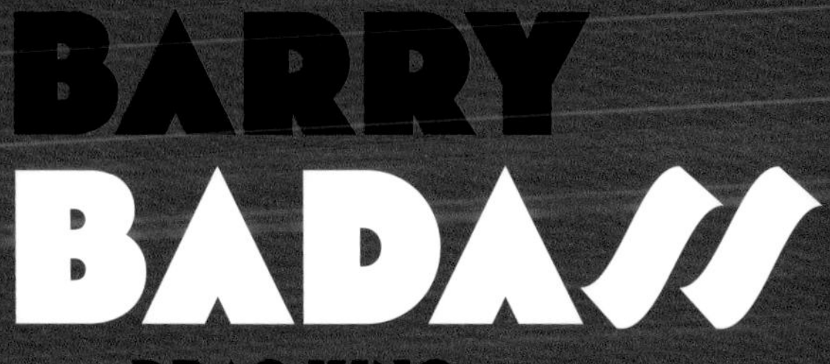


Barry Badass, the Drag King alter-ego of world record-holding circus artist Symone, is a time-travelling, smoozy, mother-fella from Chicago, and member of Pecs Drag King Collective. Born in 1960 and still stuck in 1987, Barry is a character inspired by Blacksploitation, B Movie heroes, and civil rights activists. In his world, he owns a queer cabaret club, and is a political and sensitive gendefuck who has a passion for LGBTQIA+, black, and sex worker rights. He also has a thing for guns and farmers markets.

# JACK BARROW

## MALE BURLESQUE

If Freddie Mercury and Liza Minelli had a child that ended up being as fabulous as they were, that child would be Jack Barrow. Jack is an actor, dancer, educator, producer of burlesque variety shows, good old fashioned lover boy, charming bastard, and NYC GLAM Award winner for Best Burlesque Performer.

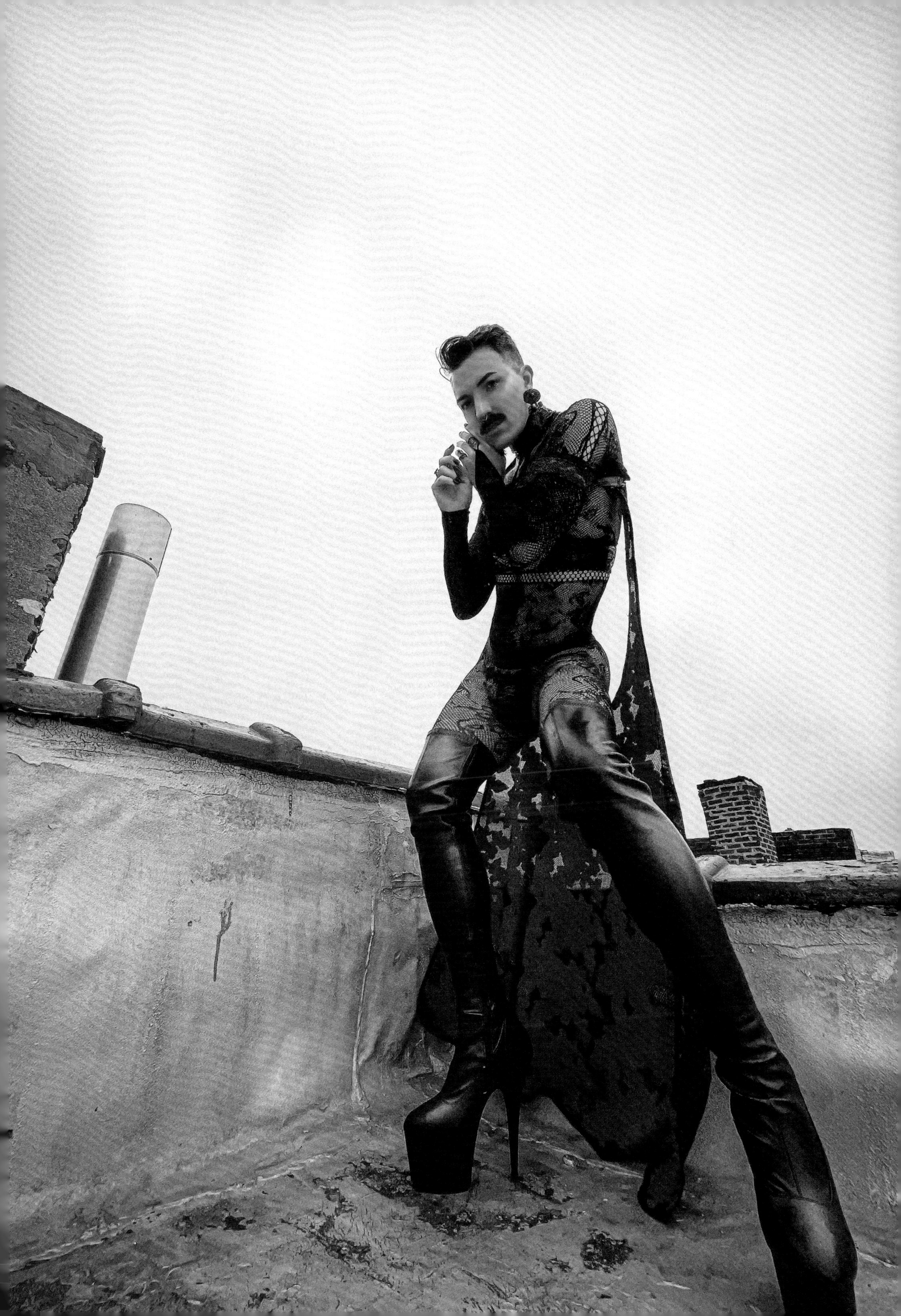

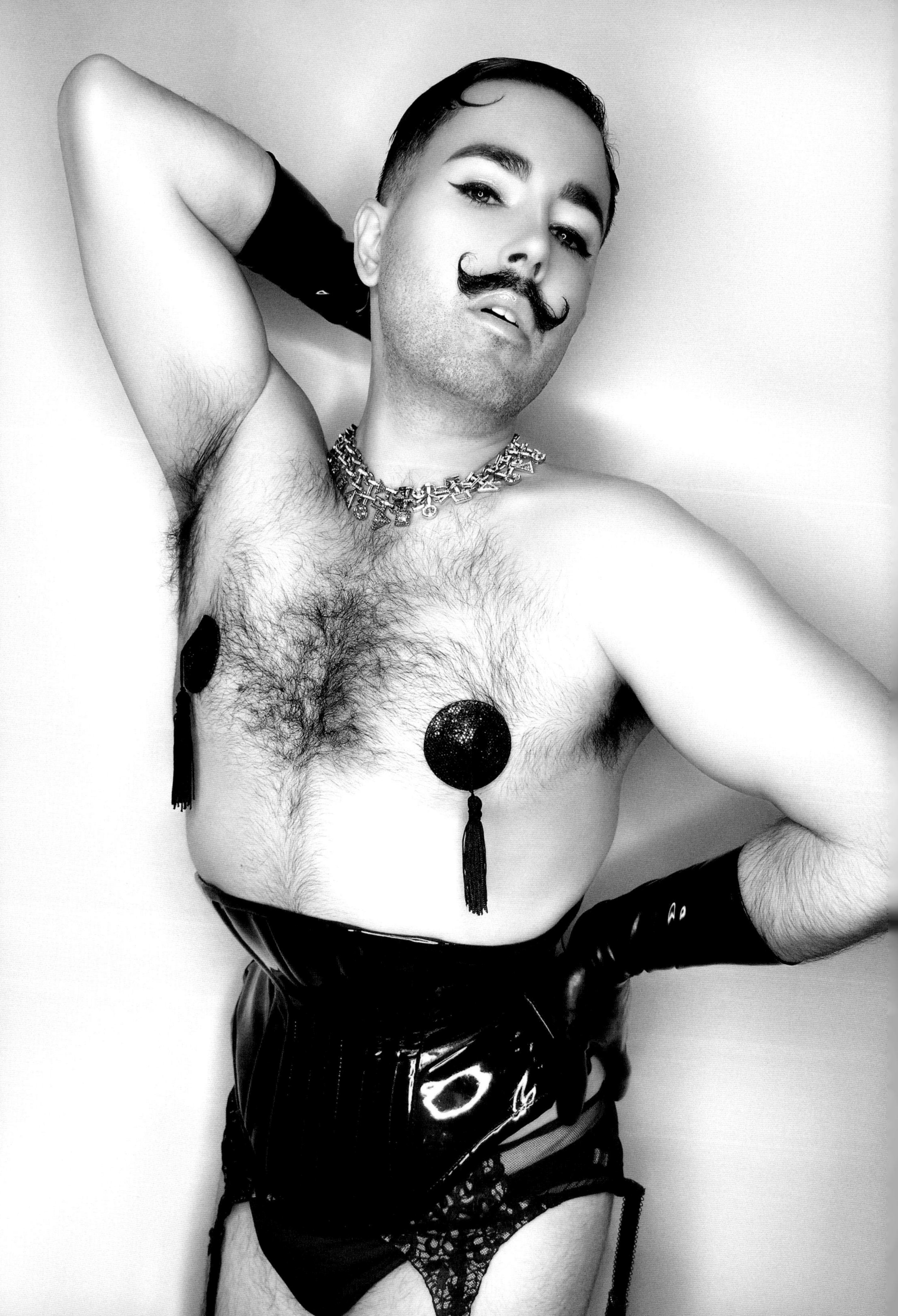

# JOHN VON TËSSE

## BOYLESQUE

John Von Tësse is a boylesque performer, erotic model, graphic designer, and photographer based in Madrid. His performances and aesthetics combine inspirations from classical burlesque icons like Dita Von Teese with a classic masculine vaudevillian charm.

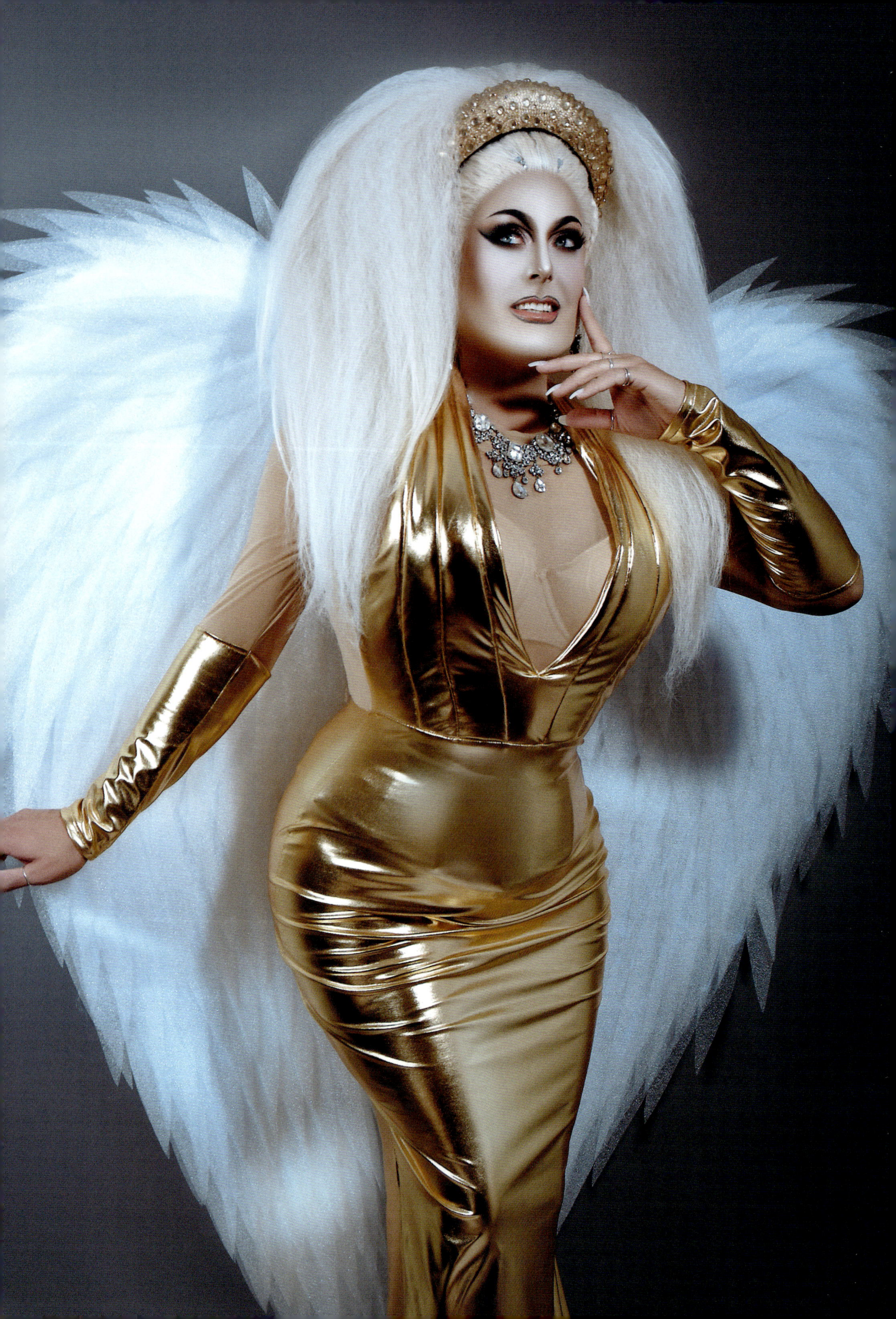

# THE
# MADAME

## DRAG QUEEN

The Madame is Kent's number one tourist attraction. With over a decade in the business and an opening (number) larger than Leeds Castle, she can be relied on for topical comedy, quick humour, and parodies that will ruin songs for you for years to come. She holds no pretentious accolades but the infamous finger licking bargain bucket is the stuff of legend among attendees of her show.

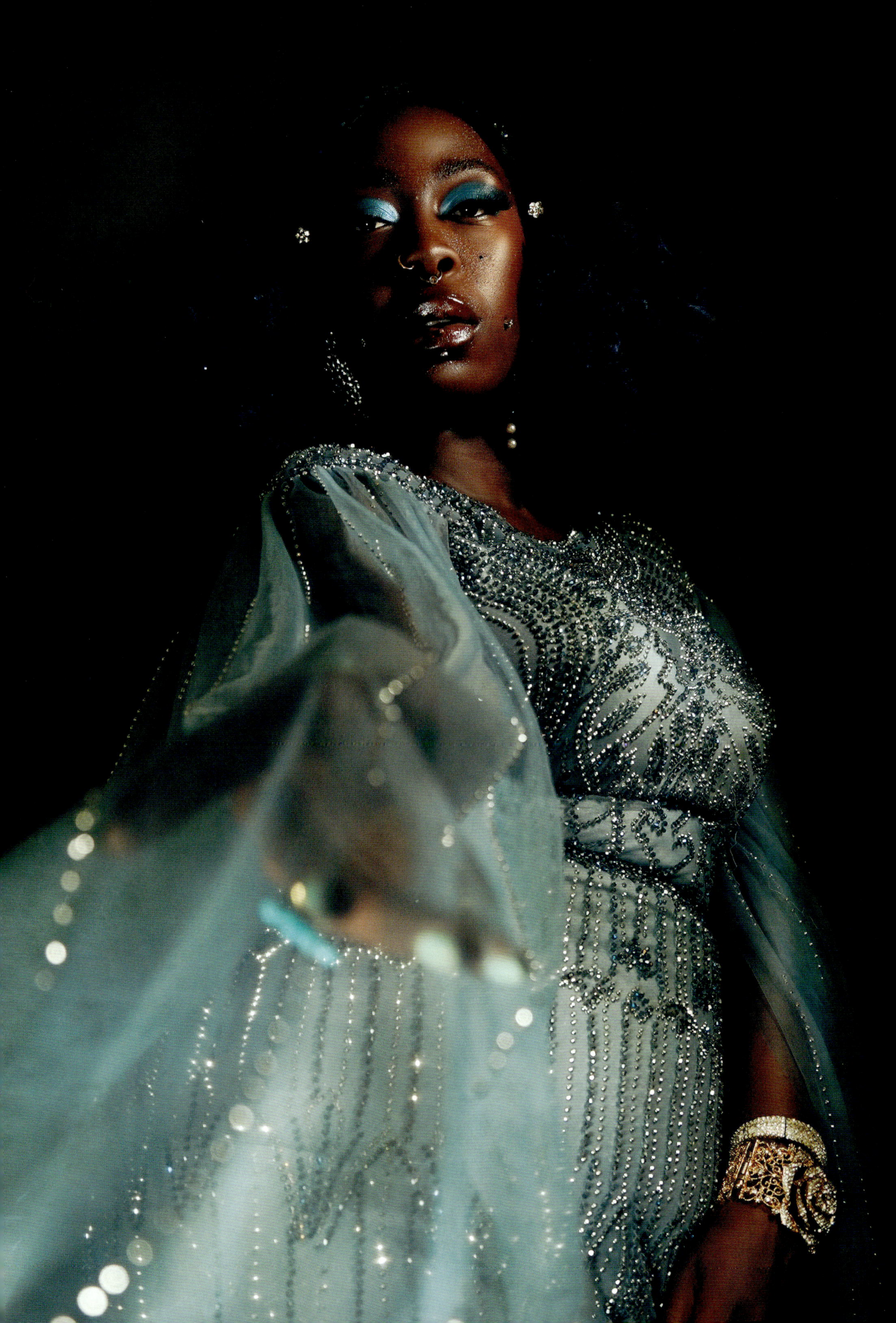

# SADIE SINNER

## CABARET COMPÈRE & SINGER

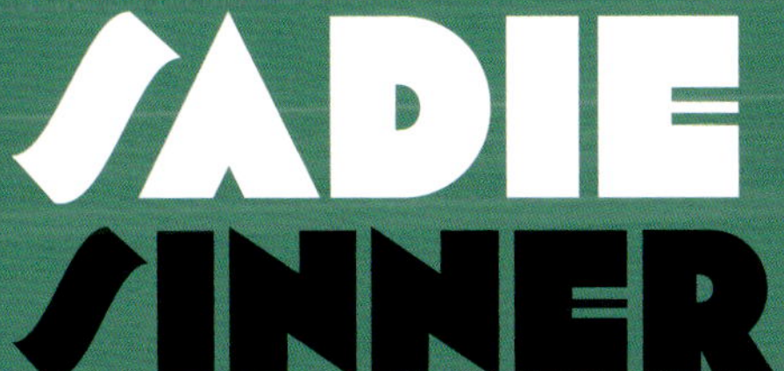

Sadie Sinner The Songbird is a creative force, and a game-changer in the UK
and international cabaret scene, having founded The Cocoa Butter Club and
The Black Burlesque School, and as curator of The Black Burlesque Revue. As
a solo performer, Sadie's vocals bring entire rooms to their feet, her seamless
repertoire of the music that raised her—R&B, Blues, Jazz, Motown, Funk, and
Neo-Soul—compelling audiences to dance the night away.

# LILLY SNATCHDRAGON

## DRAG QUEEN & BURLESQUE

"With cabaret, there's no fourth wall, so you're not looking in, you're invited to be part of it. It shows you there's more to life than what society tells you to be."

There are many parts of neo-burlesque performer, Drag Queen, compère, and producer Lilly SnatchDragon's identity that have made her journey in the cabaret world unique and, at times, challenging to maneuver. But in the same breath, they've also made her the representation that many need.

Internationally known for her innovative brand of political comedy and performances that explore Western stereotypes of Asian women like herself, Lilly SnatchDragon doesn't shy away from the qualities that make her inevitably stand out, embodying a fearless, feminine, and outspoken persona that releases her from the shackles and stories the world has placed onto her.

As well as being an award-winning solo performer, she is also a co-founder of the Bitten Peach, a ground-breaking pan-Asian cabaret collective.

Lilly believes that cabaret, burlesque, and drag filled in a missing piece of her. It allowed her to come to terms with her identity and find her place in the world. She sees cabaret as an escape, and also as something that can open minds and help people to imagine how things could be. She wishes that people knew just how rich a world cabaret is and that what people see on the television barely scratches the surface.

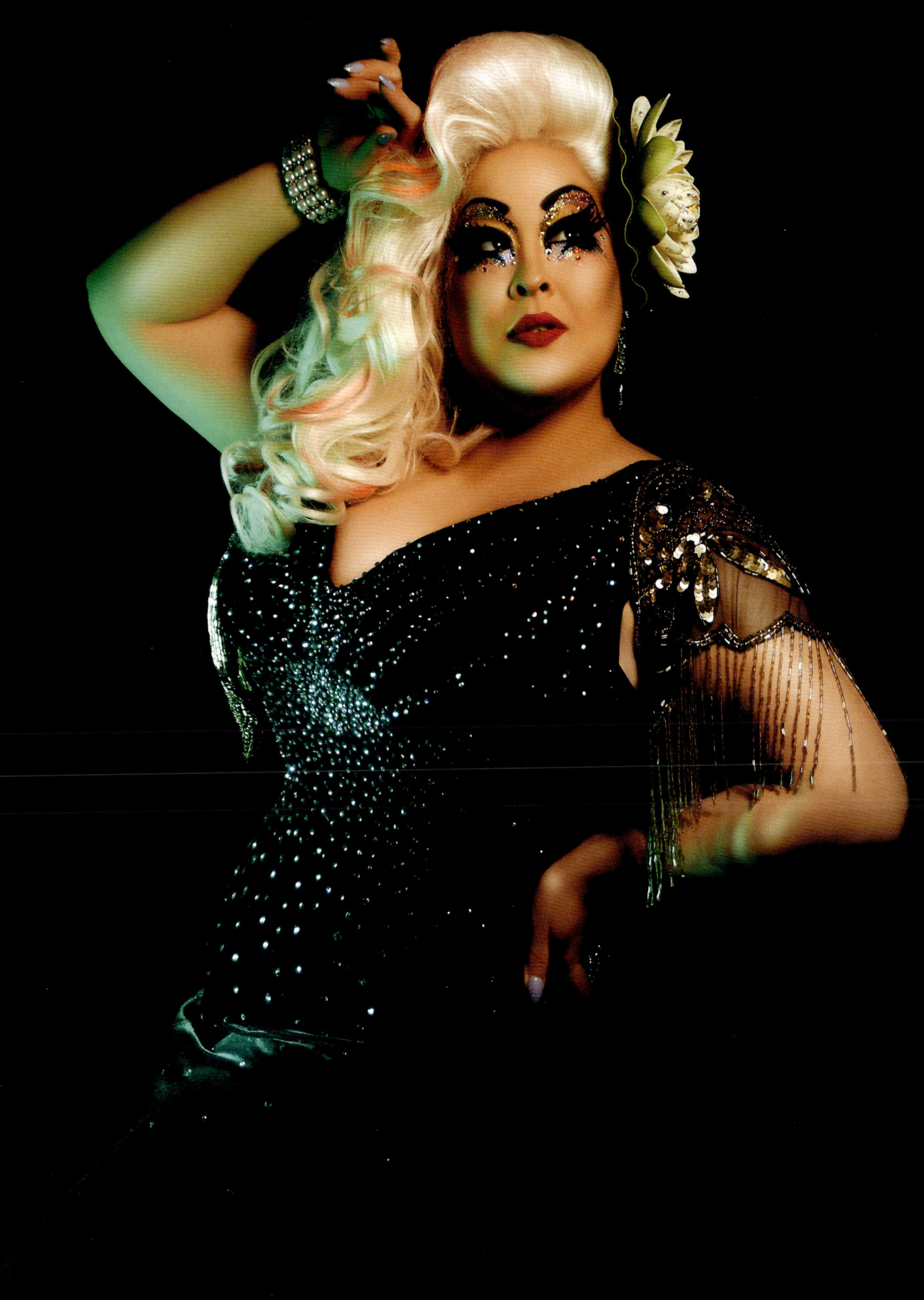

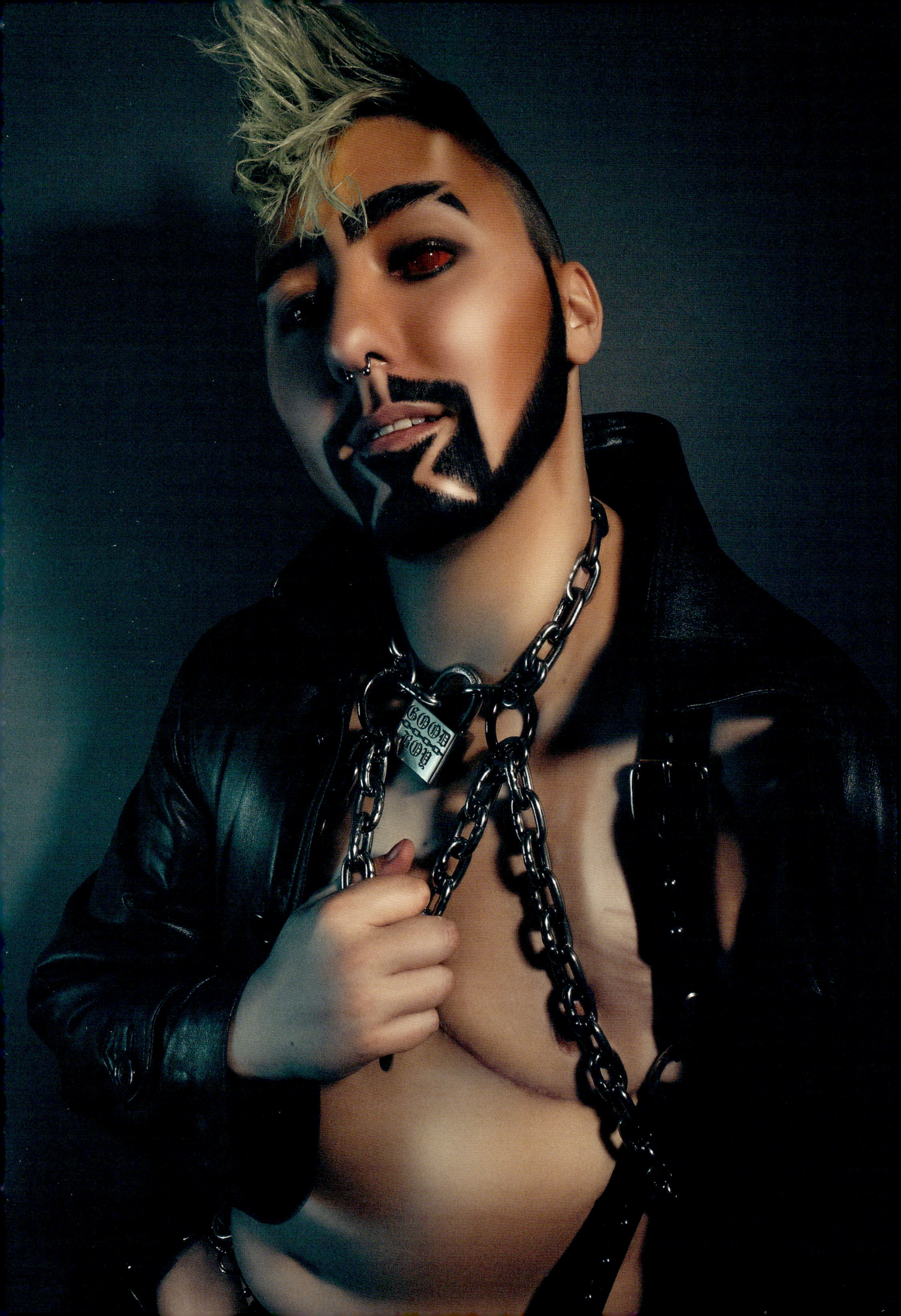
GOOD
BOY

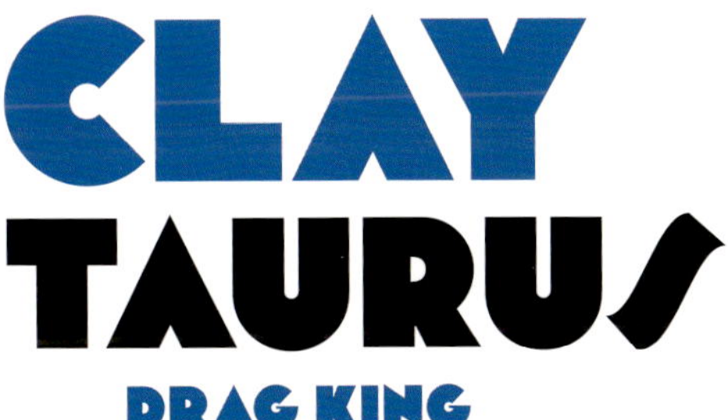

# CLAY TAURUS

## DRAG KING

Clay Taurus is primarily a mover and a lip-syncer. He loves to play with different genres and styles in his performances. While largely leaning toward more alternative aesthetics and inspirations, drag is a playground for him to explore and celebrate his gender and presentation. His performances allow him the flexibility to be whoever and whatever he wants on any given night.

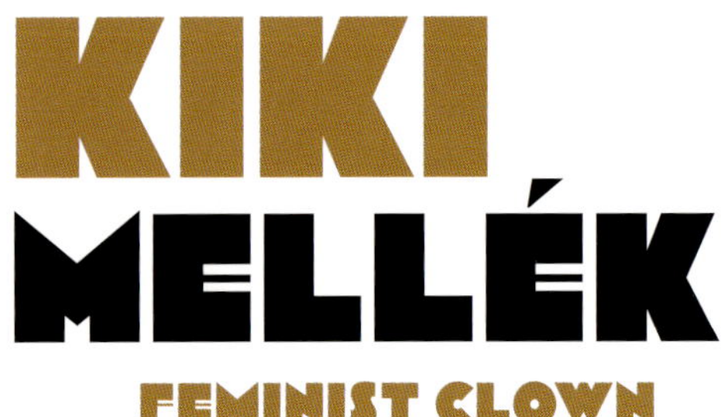

# KIKI MELLÉK
## FEMINIST CLOWN

Kiki Mellék is a professional actor with a love for satirical character comedy.
Kiki is a Feminist Clown, a phantasmagorical character with an extreme aesthetic.
She never blends in, thrives on attention, and lives for all things Kiki.

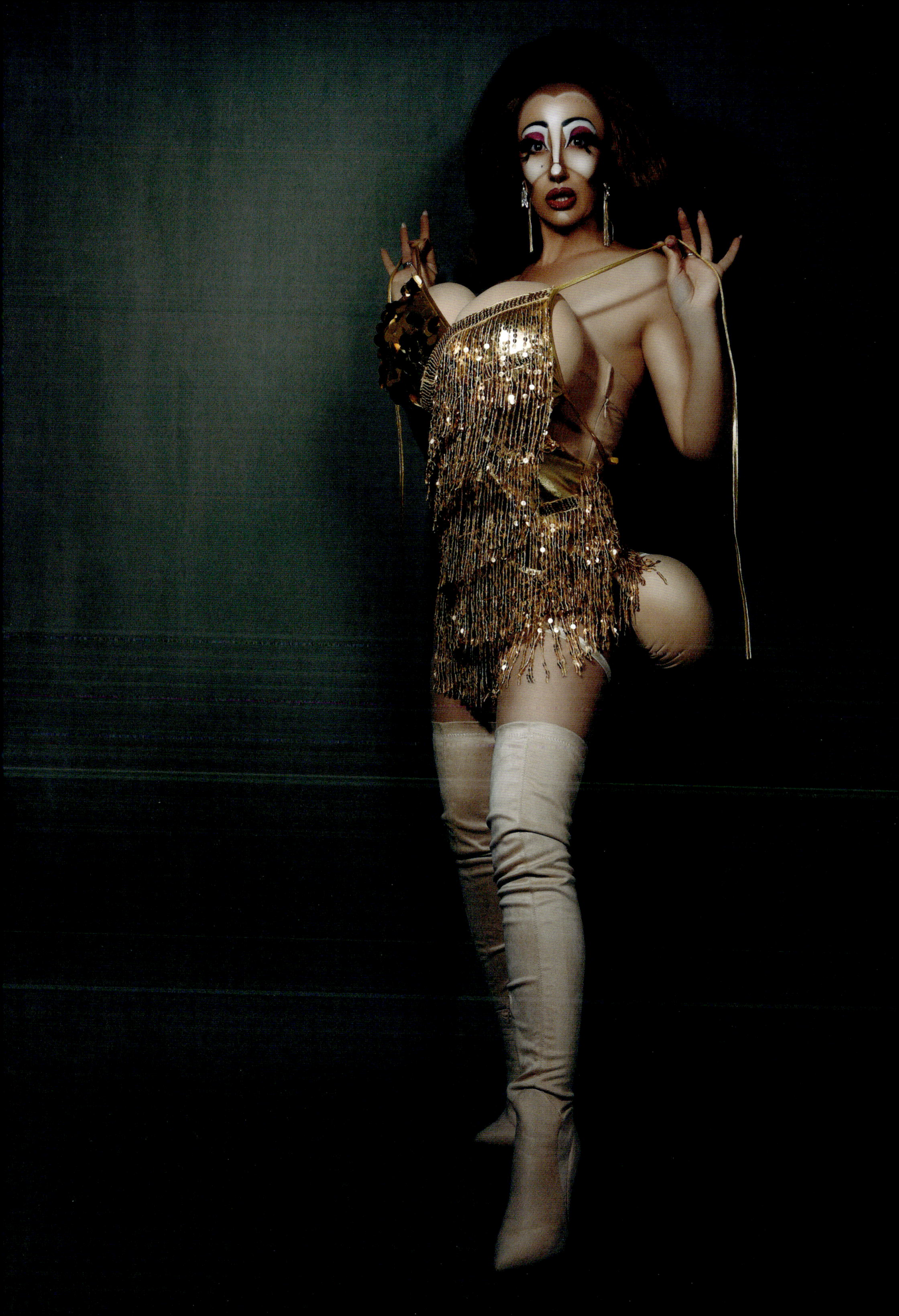

"When I was 11 years old, my teacher had a backstage pass for the touring theatre production Die Nacht der Musicals. That night, I promised myself I would become a performer."

# MELANCHOLIA BLACKBILE

## QUEERLESQUE & DRAGLESQUE

Melancholia Blackbile is an international Queer showghoul, producer of Blackbile Productions, trans male actor, and androgynous model. Originally from Australia and now based in Prague, Melancholia's acts combine drag, burlesque, and circus skills, drawing from a love of performance art, horror, and burlesque elegance.

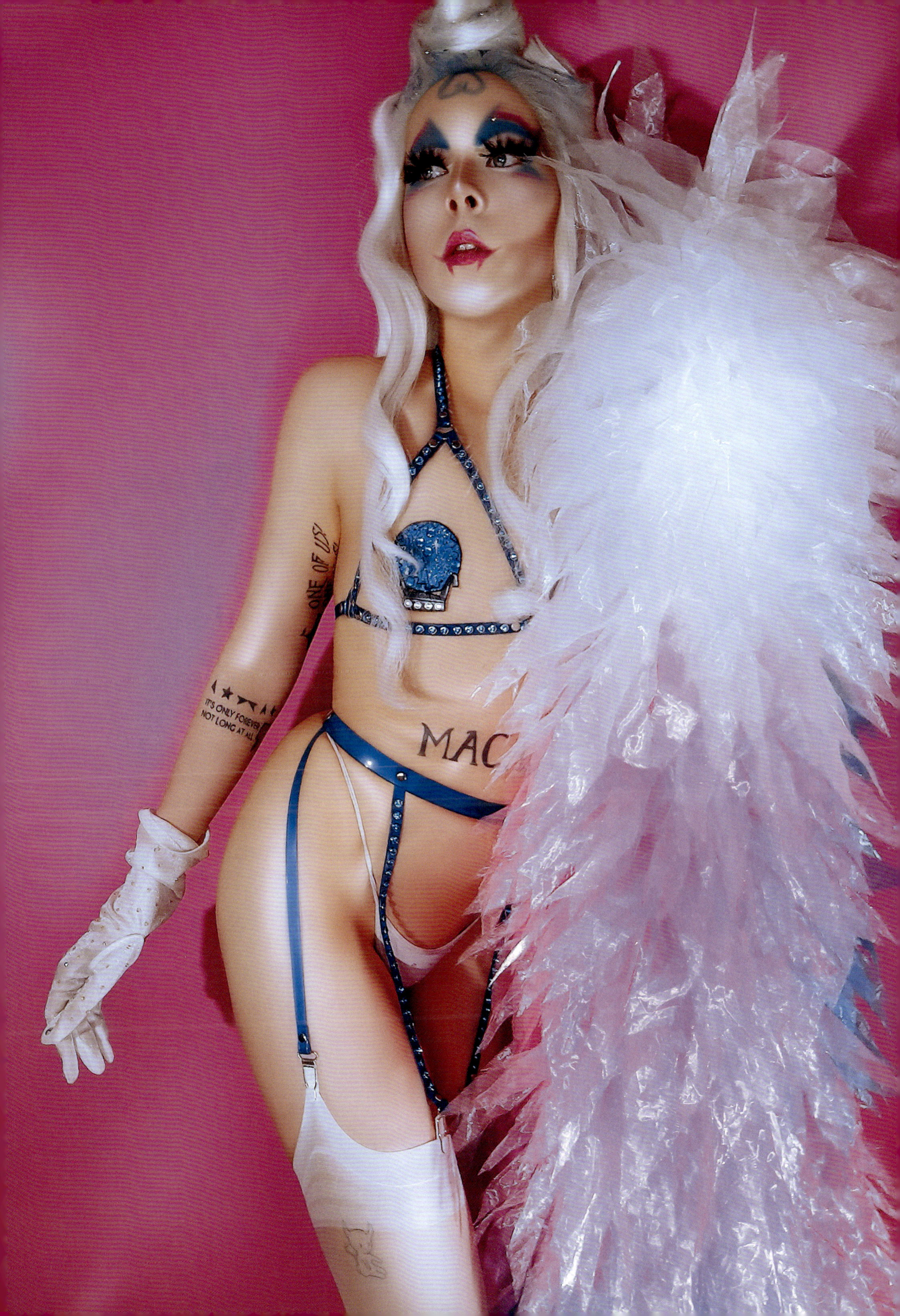

ONE OF US
IT'S ONLY FOREVER
NOT LONG AT ALL
MAC

# EVELYN CARNATE
## BURLESQUE & QUEERLESQUE

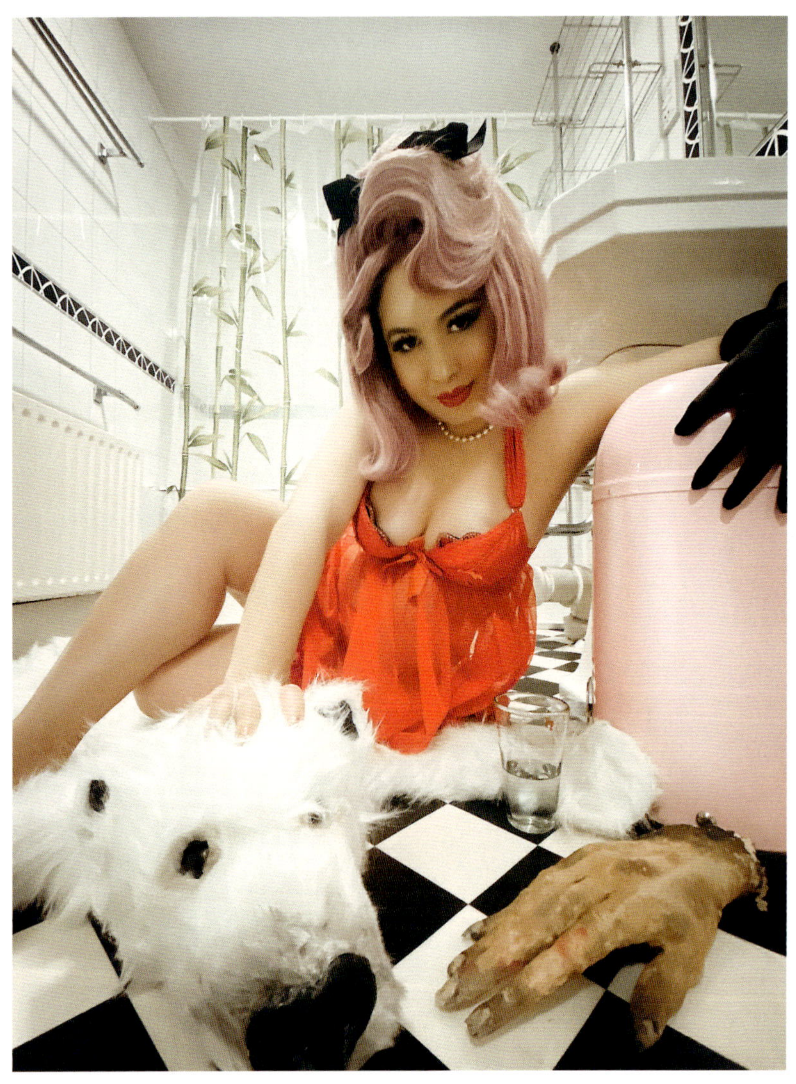

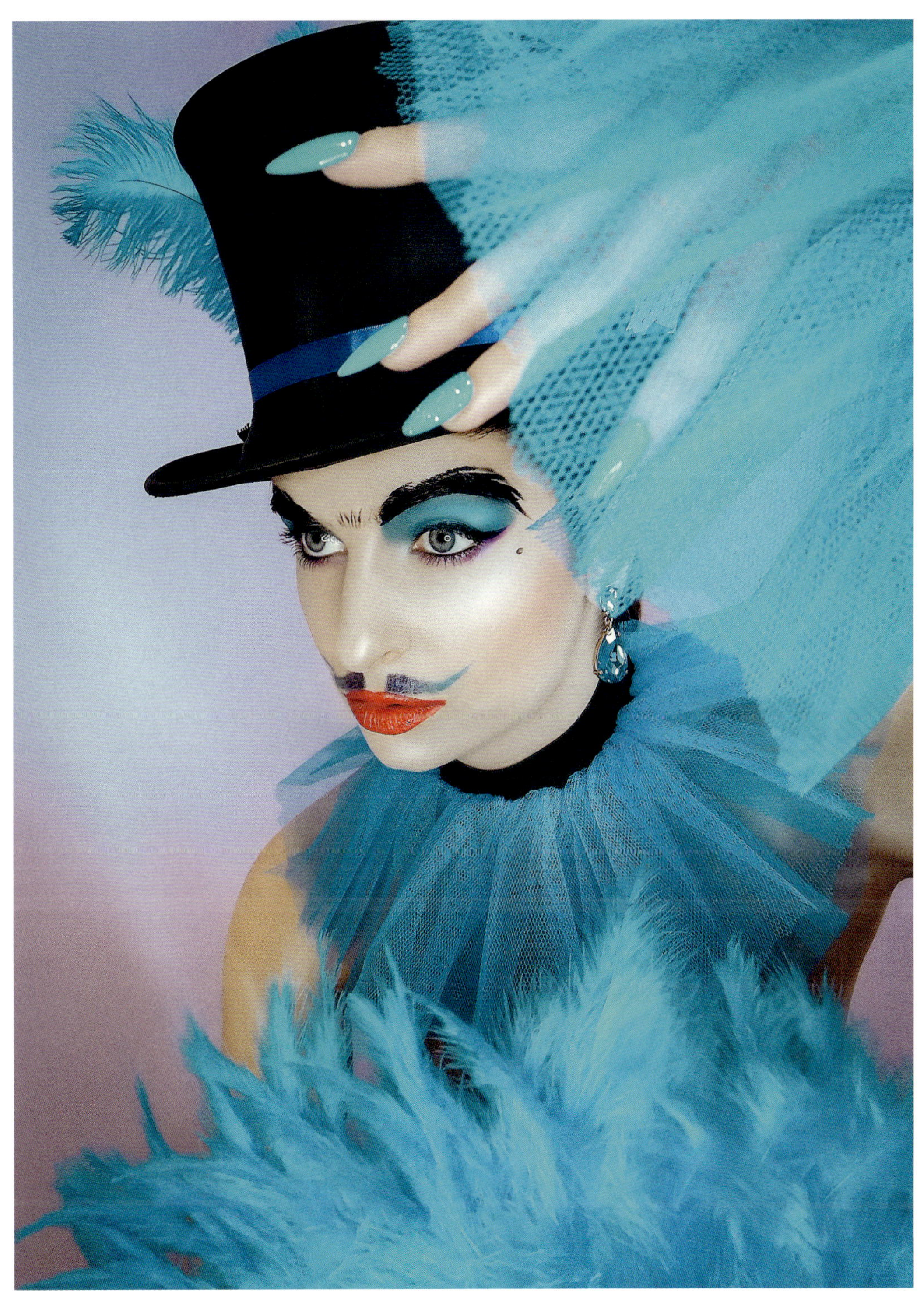

# VALENTINA LETALE
## BURLESQUE & DRAG

# MISS TERRI BOXX

## DRAG QUEEN

Miss Terri Boxx is a bearded drag queen with a style that blends spooky and
sexy. Their performances are powerful, sensual, and breathtakingly high-energy.
Give them a stage and they'll use every inch of it.

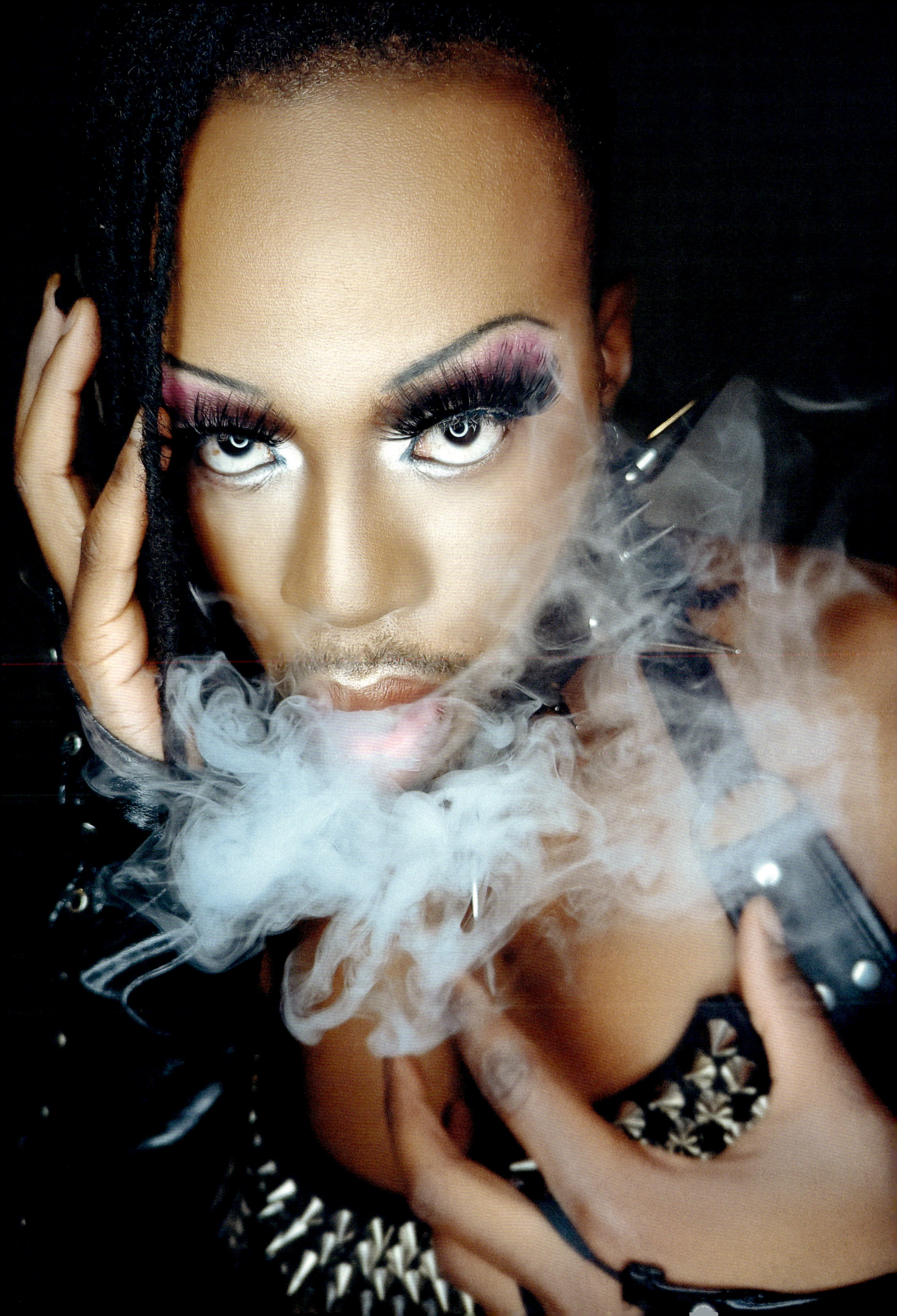

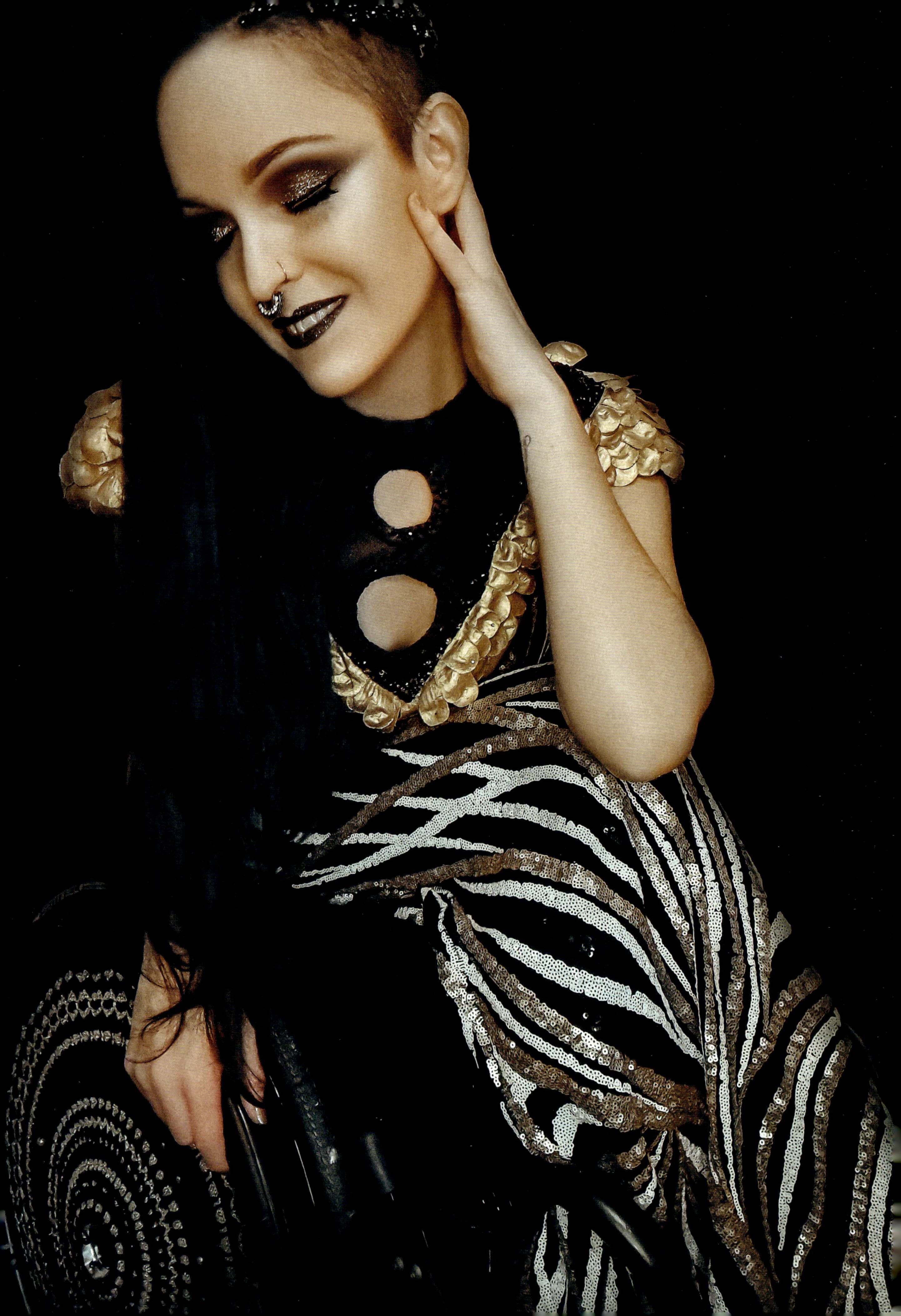

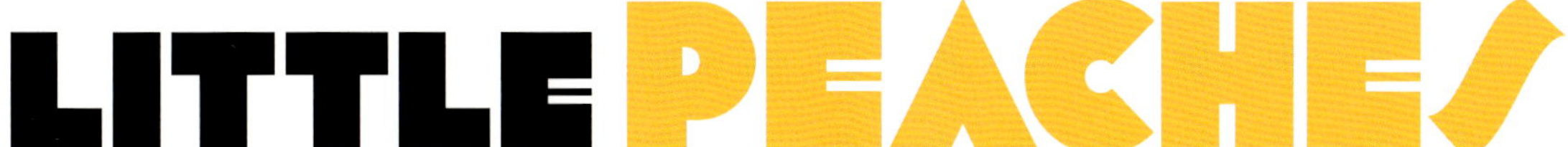

# LITTLE PEACHES

## BURLESQUE & QUEERLESQUE

> "It's my way to tell the world that disabled people are sexual, sensual, talented beings worthy of having their voices heard and deserving of cabaret stages."

Little Peaches, a burlesque and queerlesque performer, was advised to stop dancing when she was diagnosed with Ehlers Danlos Syndrome, but the warning instead motivated her to sign up for burlesque classes the following day. Performing for Little Peaches means being free, and she believes those moments on stage are meant for celebration and protest. Her performances are poignant and political, exploring the strength and vulnerability with which she navigates the world as a queer, disabled performer.

Little Peaches uses her career to advocate for more accessibility in her industry. Many of the venues where shows are held do not accommodate those with disabilities, making it difficult for performers to put on their best shows, or even access the space at all, and for audience members with disabilities to attend.

One of her proudest moments was the debut of her own show, DisabiliTease, in 2019, which provided a platform for disabled performers. She also hoped to provide the performers the confidence to own this part of their identity since many were afraid to admit their disability out of fear of not being booked.

Having twice been named one of the world's top 50 Most Influential Burlesque Performers and invited to compete at the legendary Burlesque Hall of Fame in Las Vegas in 2023, Little Peaches is a force to be reckoned with.

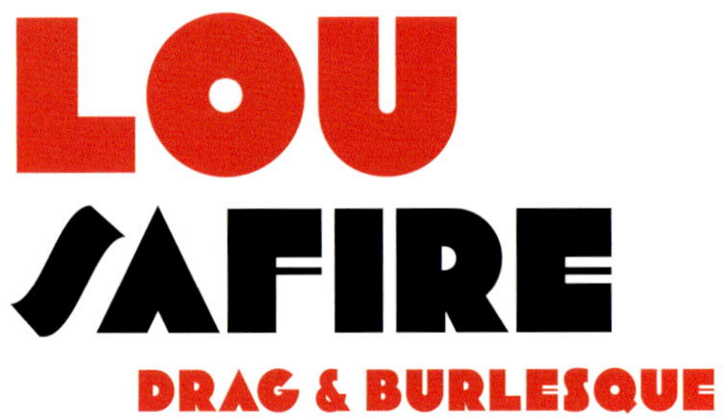


Born somewhere between London and Hell, international vaudevillian Lou Safire has been strutting their stuff around the world since 2008, combining classical burlesque with the darker side of Vaudeville. Lou specialises in unusual burlesque projects with a bohemian streak, often incorporating circus skills, fire, and traditional freak show stunts.

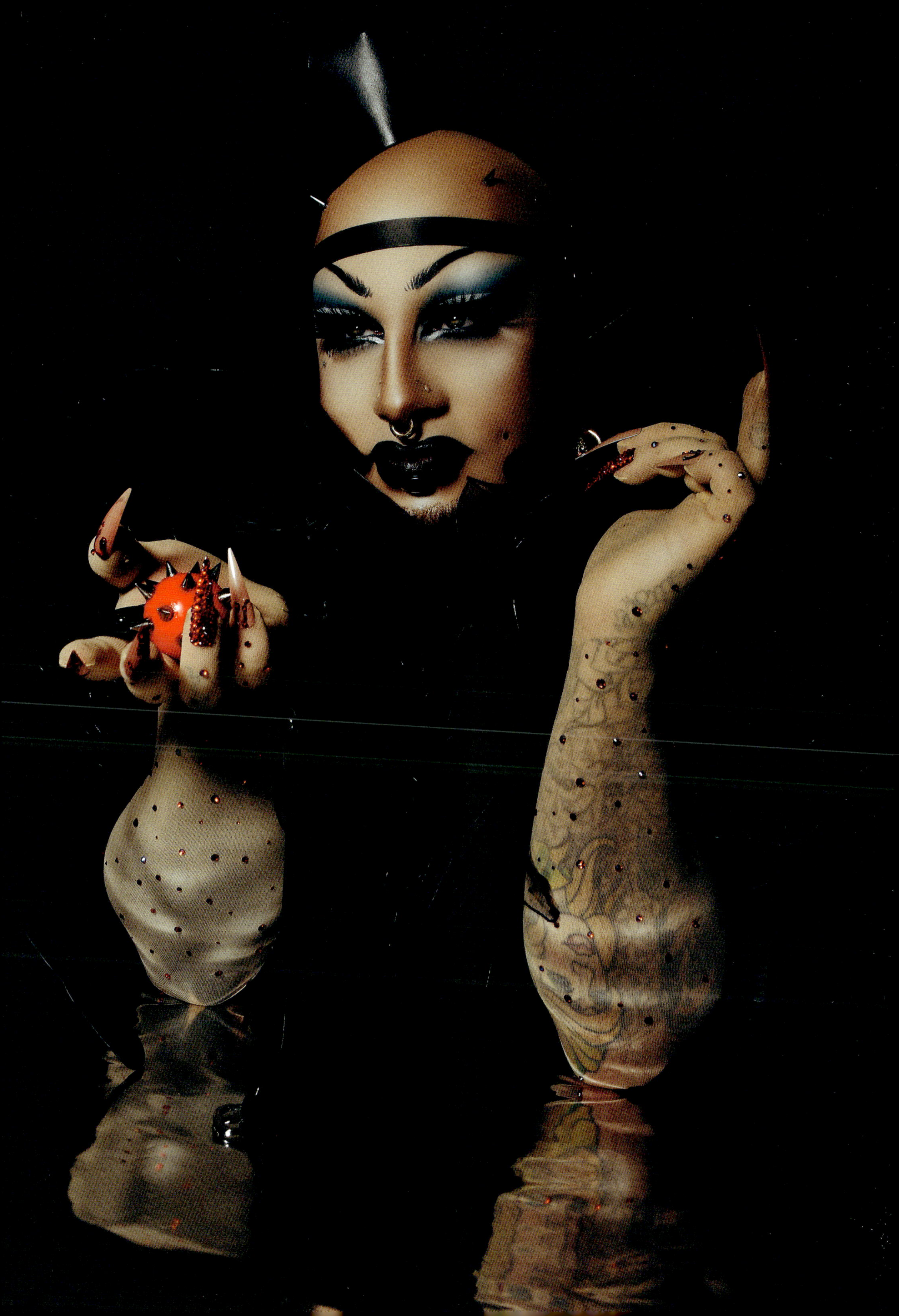

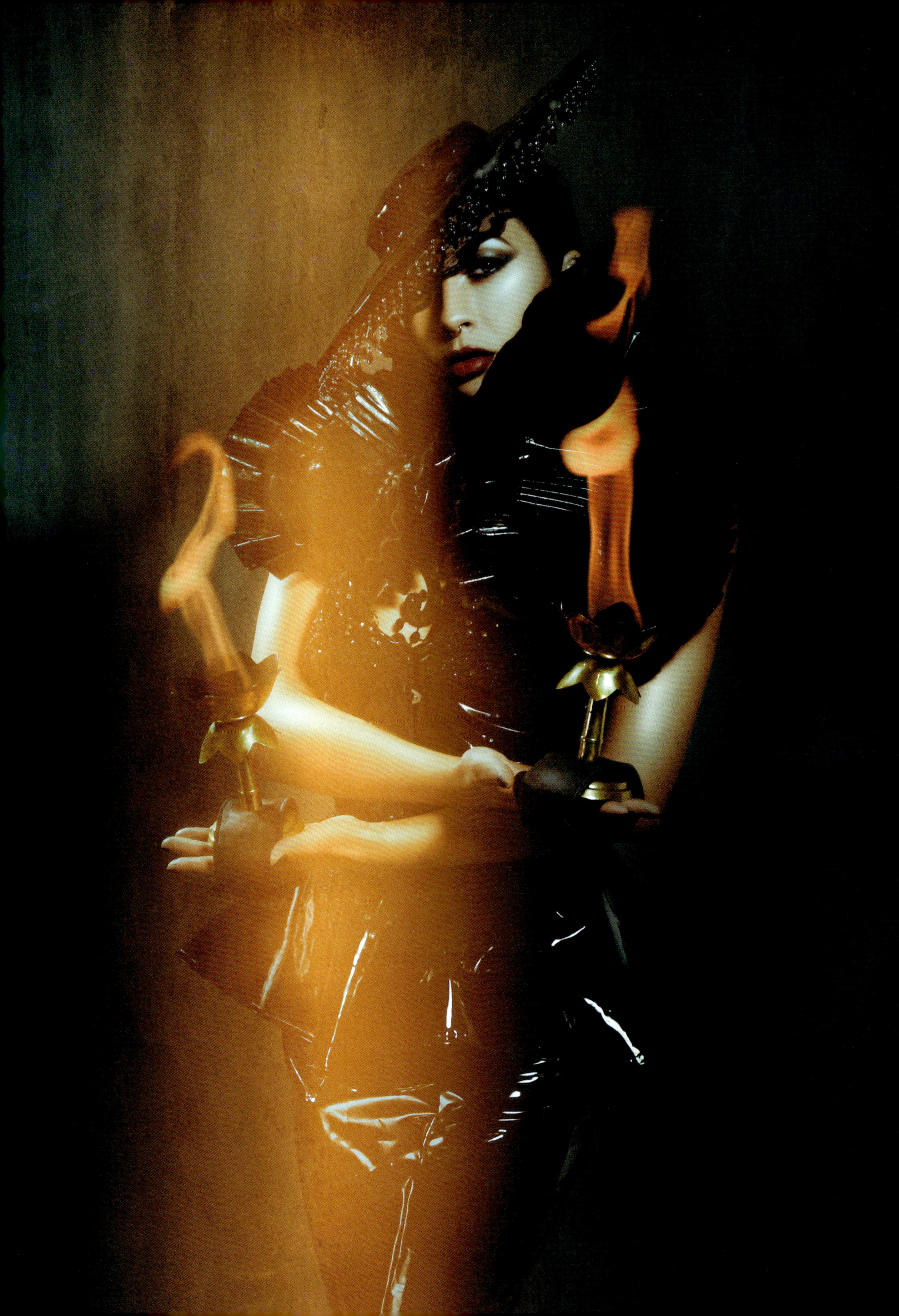

# AURORA STARR

## BURLESQUE & CIRCUS

Including circus, burlesque, aerial, fire, and swords, Aurora Starr's list of skills is seemingly endless. Merging these multiple stage crafts with a mesmerising sensuality and opulent aesthetic, she has taken her unique blend of danger and decadence to stages around the world.

"An evening at a cabaret can be many things, the excitement is in the unknowing. I can go to a cabaret show and see joyful silliness and beautiful art, a mixture of darkness, light, and light in the darkness."

# RUBY WEDNESDAY

## DRAG THING & MUSICIAN

Ruby Wednesday is a formidably talented and somewhat indefinable musician, cabaret artist and occasional drag creature, co-producer of RiffRaff Kabarett, and creator of award-winning stage show Narcissus, based on their poetry and the music of their debut album. With over a decade in the cabaret scene, Ruby is an utterly captivating performer with haunting, forceful vocals, a scathing wit, and a fearless honesty that always leaves an audience firmly in their grip.

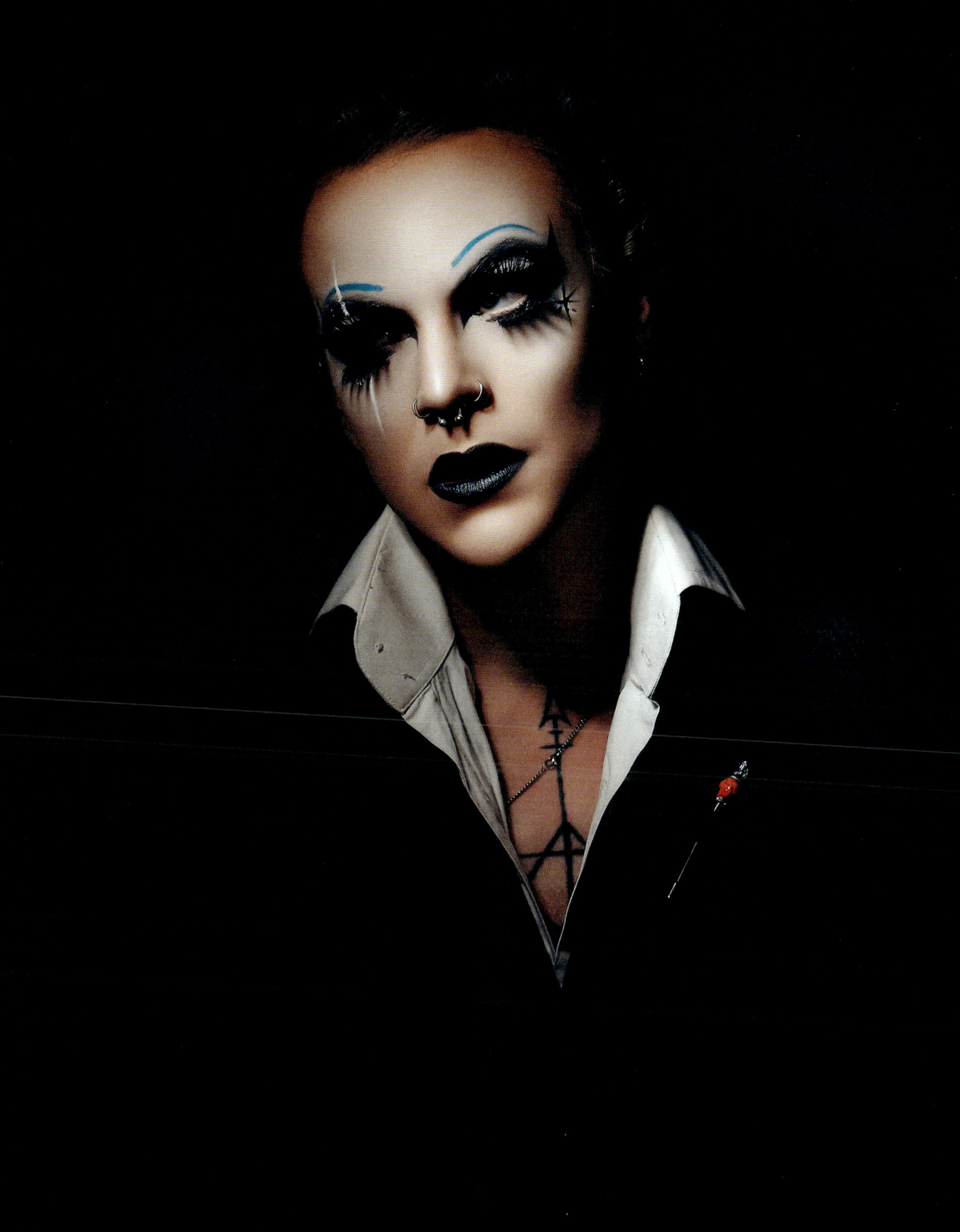

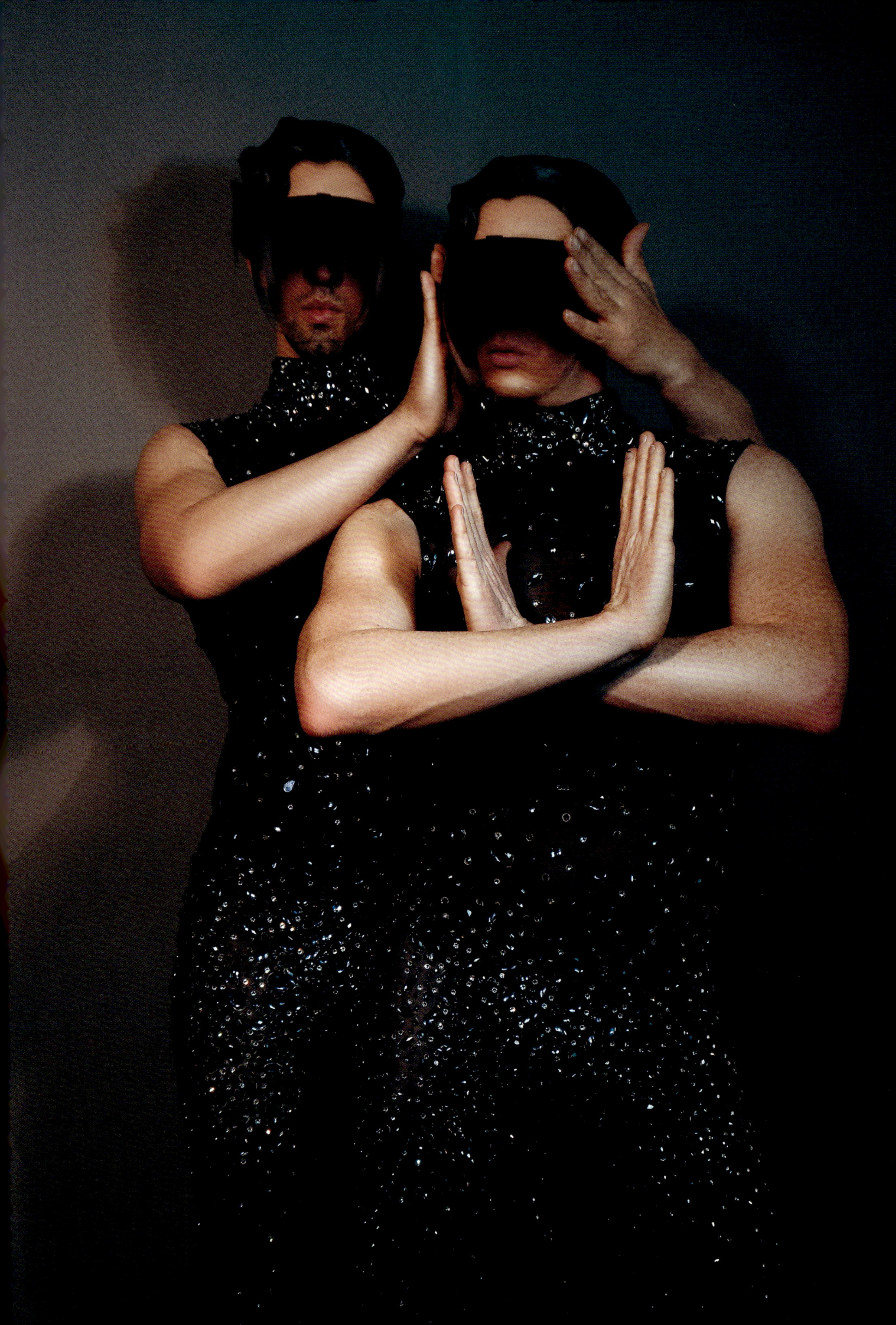

# DUO LITTLE FINCH

## QUEERLESQUE & QUEER CIRCUS

Little Finch are an international aerial duo who have amazed audiences on some of the biggest stages in the world, like the Friedrichstadt Palast in Berlin and *France's Got Talent*, as well as renowned fashion houses Jean Paul Gaultier and Dolce & Gabbana. Residing where Circus meets fashion, their acts are a mix of skilled aerial artistry, drag, boylesque, comedy, and haute couture.

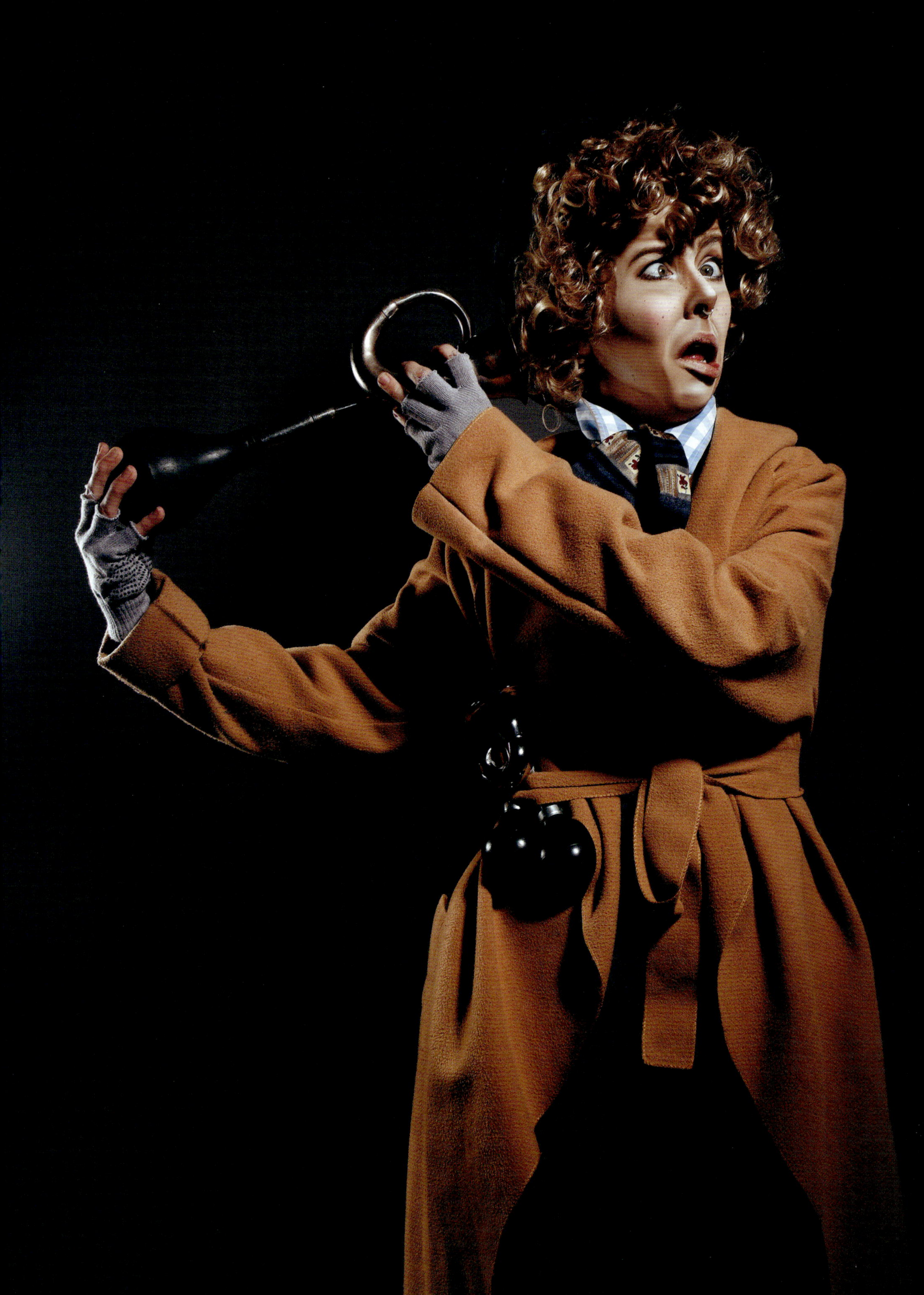

**"**To quote the great Amanda Lepore: 'I just show up all done up, dance, do my thing, get paid and I'm out.'**"**

# VICAR'S DAUGHTER
## DRAG SWING (KING/QUEEN/IN-BETWEEN)

The Vicar's Daughter is a Sunday School dropout with one eye on heaven and one hand in the collection plate. The UK's primary non-binary Drag Swing, they perform as a King, Queen, and everything beyond and between. They play all the parts, putting themselves in the shoes of others to make sense of themselves and the world around them.

"The moment that made me choose to become a cabaret performer was meeting Judith Stein and Ophelia Flame backstage at the Best of the Midwest Burlesque Festival. That conversation gave me permission to take a chance on myself and invest in something that would bring me joy and happiness."

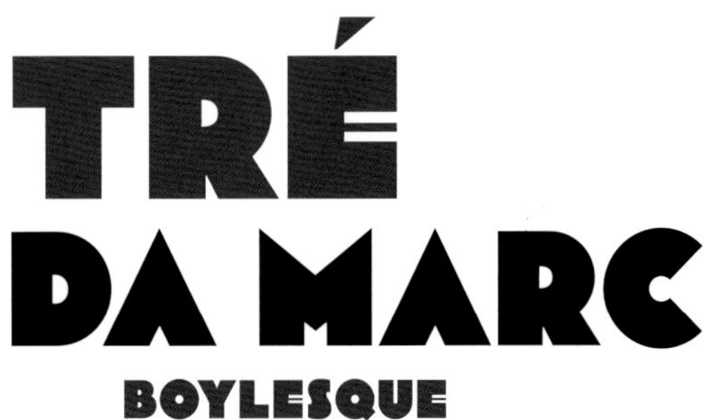


The Chocolate Drop That Won't Stop, Tré Da Marc is an international boylesque sensation hailing from Minneapolis. A member of Black Hearts Burlesque and the 2020 Noire Pageant King of Burlesque, he's ready to stamp his trademark sass and ass on any stage he meets.

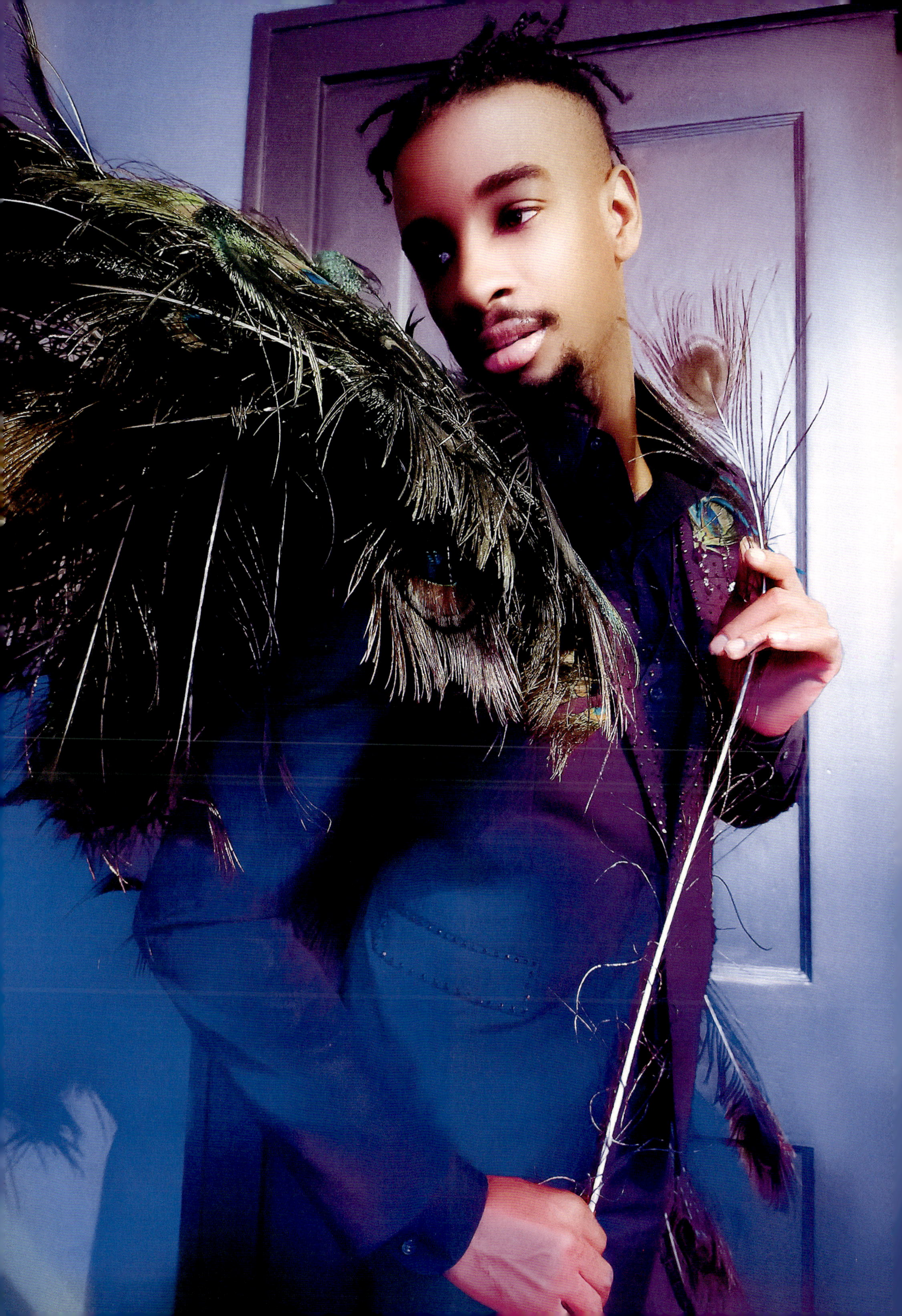

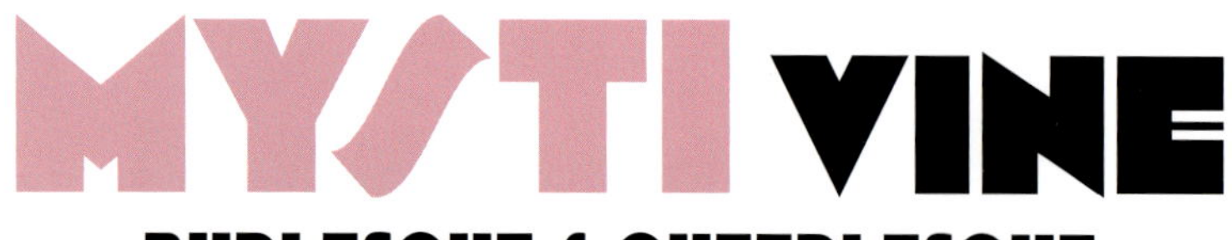


"When you hire a performer, you're hiring their experience, their hours of time spent costuming, their rehearsal times, their creative ideas that they bring to life. You don't just jump on stage fully formed—it takes time."

Mysti Vine began performing as a young child and took part in all her church presentations and school plays, exploring comedy and improv before falling into the less restrictive artforms of cabaret and burlesque. Sharing stages with some of burlesque's greatest luminaries, including Dita Von Teese, Satan's Angel, and Catherine D'Lish, Mysti's acts are as comedic and uplifting as they are sensual, and on the mic, she brings a quick wit and charming warmth that is eagerly welcomed by cabaret audiences.

Despite experiencing multiple barriers throughout her career, including sexism, ageism, and colourism, Mysti has managed to make a name for herself in the cabaret world. She believes that integrity and inclusivity go hand in hand and that if people in the industry were more forthcoming about their experiences, it would go a long way towards creating a safer and more inclusive scene. When producing shows, Mysti prioritises accessible spaces, performer safety, and inclusive line-ups, recommending performers that may not be on the radar of producers.

For Mysti, performing is how she connects with other human beings. It's a connection, she believes, that has the power to show that ultimately, we're all human, with the same wants, desires, and struggles.

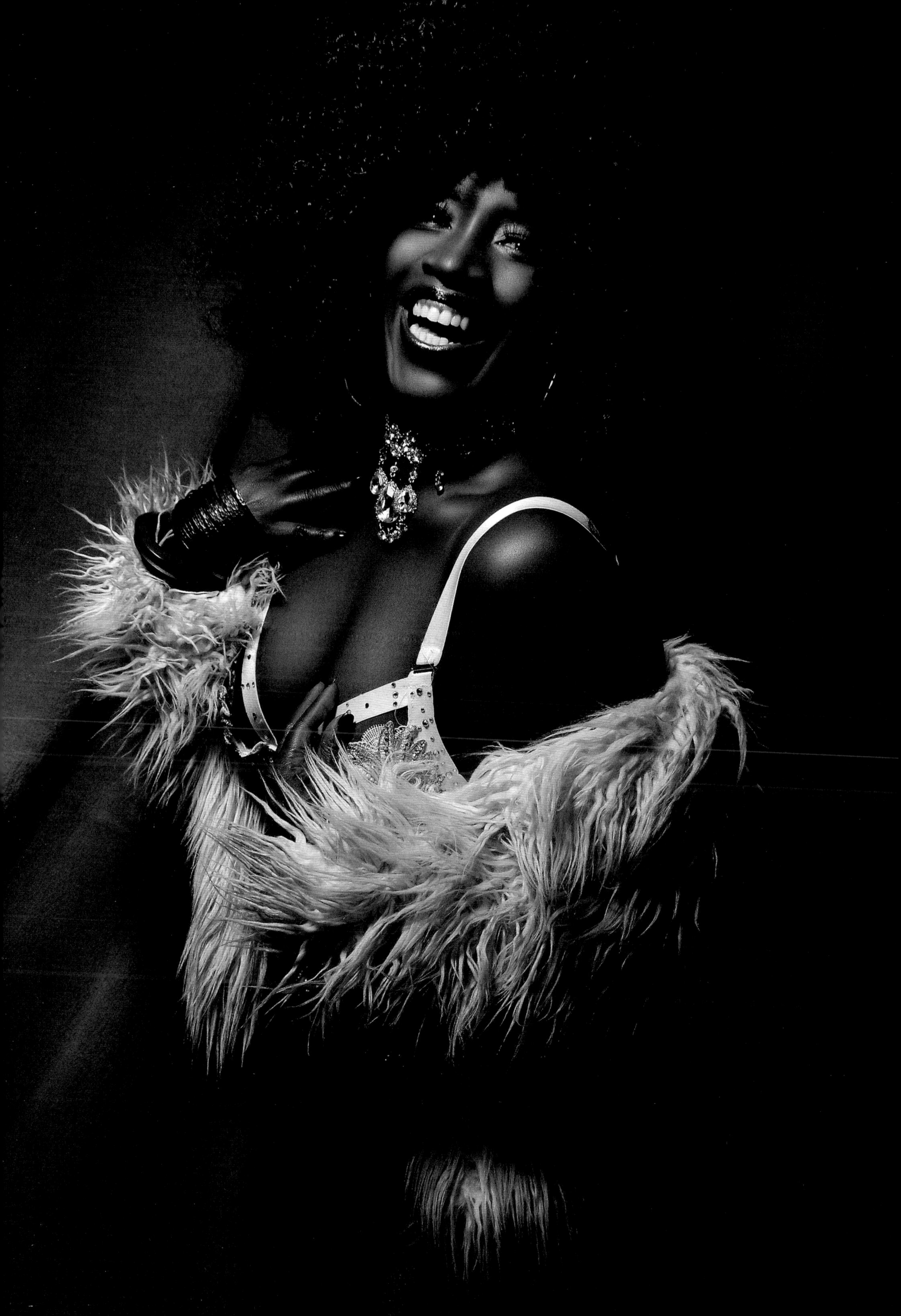

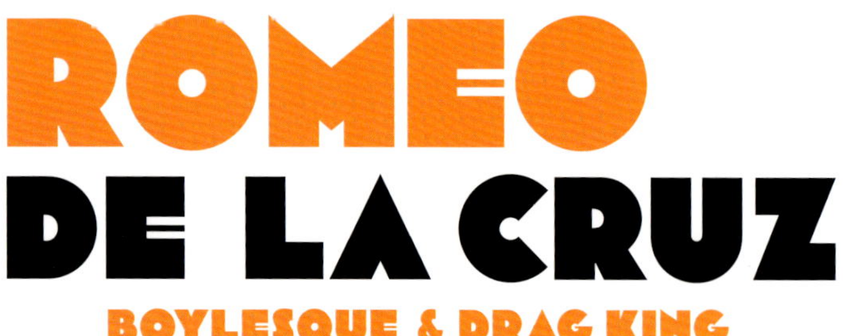

# ROMEO DE LA CRUZ

## BOYLESQUE & DRAG KING

The original Drag Kxng and Bxylesque underdog, Romeo de la Cruz is an enigmatic and scintillating performer whose acts are fuelled by experimental and extemporised dance, acting, comedy, kink, and political impact.

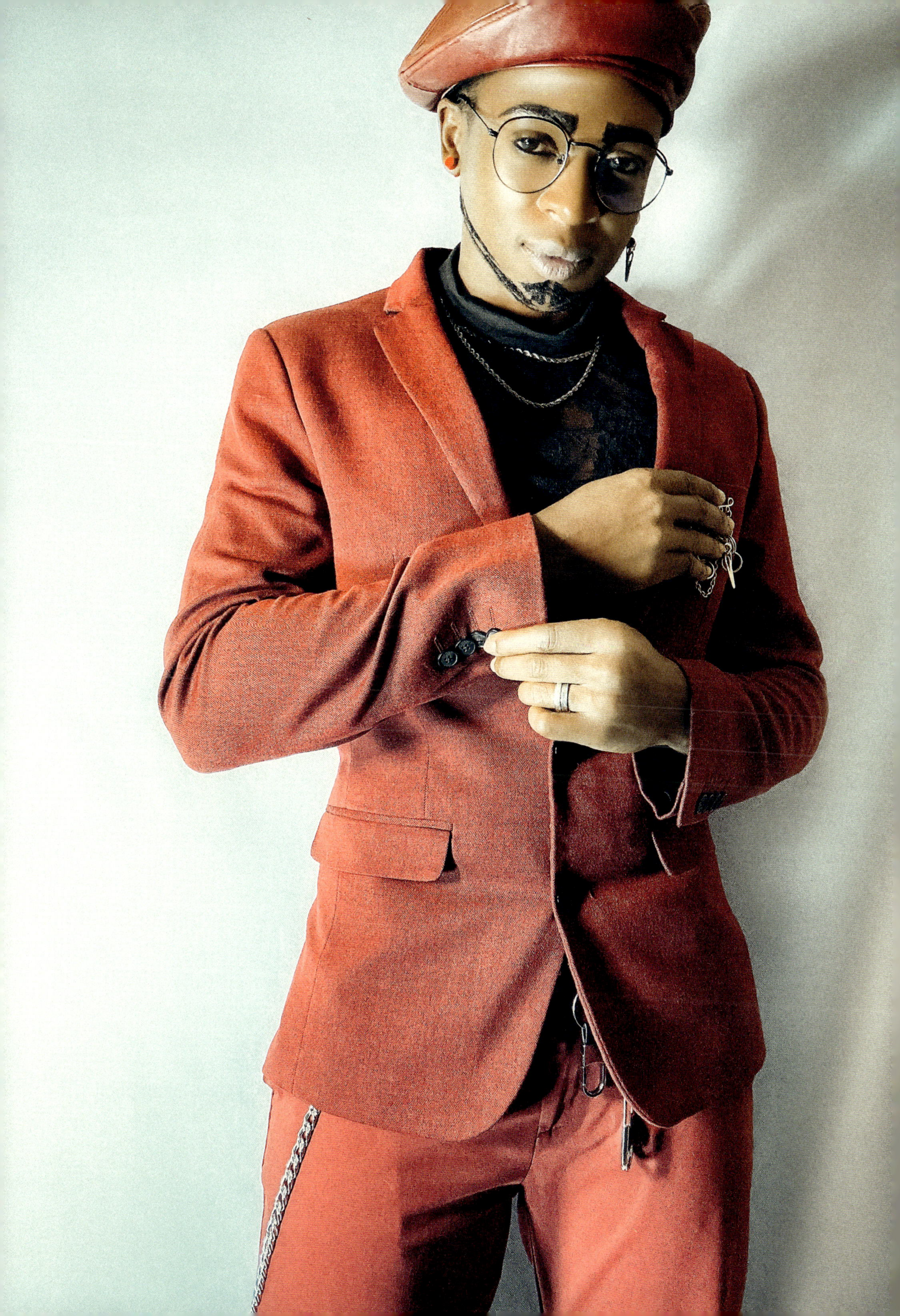

"The first time I performed burlesque was for a dare.
The audience went crazy and I was hooked right
then and there."

# GOODTIME MAMA JOJO

## BURLESQUE

British burlesque legend Goodtime Mama Jojo has been entertaining audiences
since 1978. Her effortless sensuality, vibrant personality, and tongue-in-cheek
humour catapulted her to popularity in the vibrant West End clubs of the 1980s
and 90s. She is also the founder of the UK's first burlesque and striptease school,
the London Academy of Burlesque.

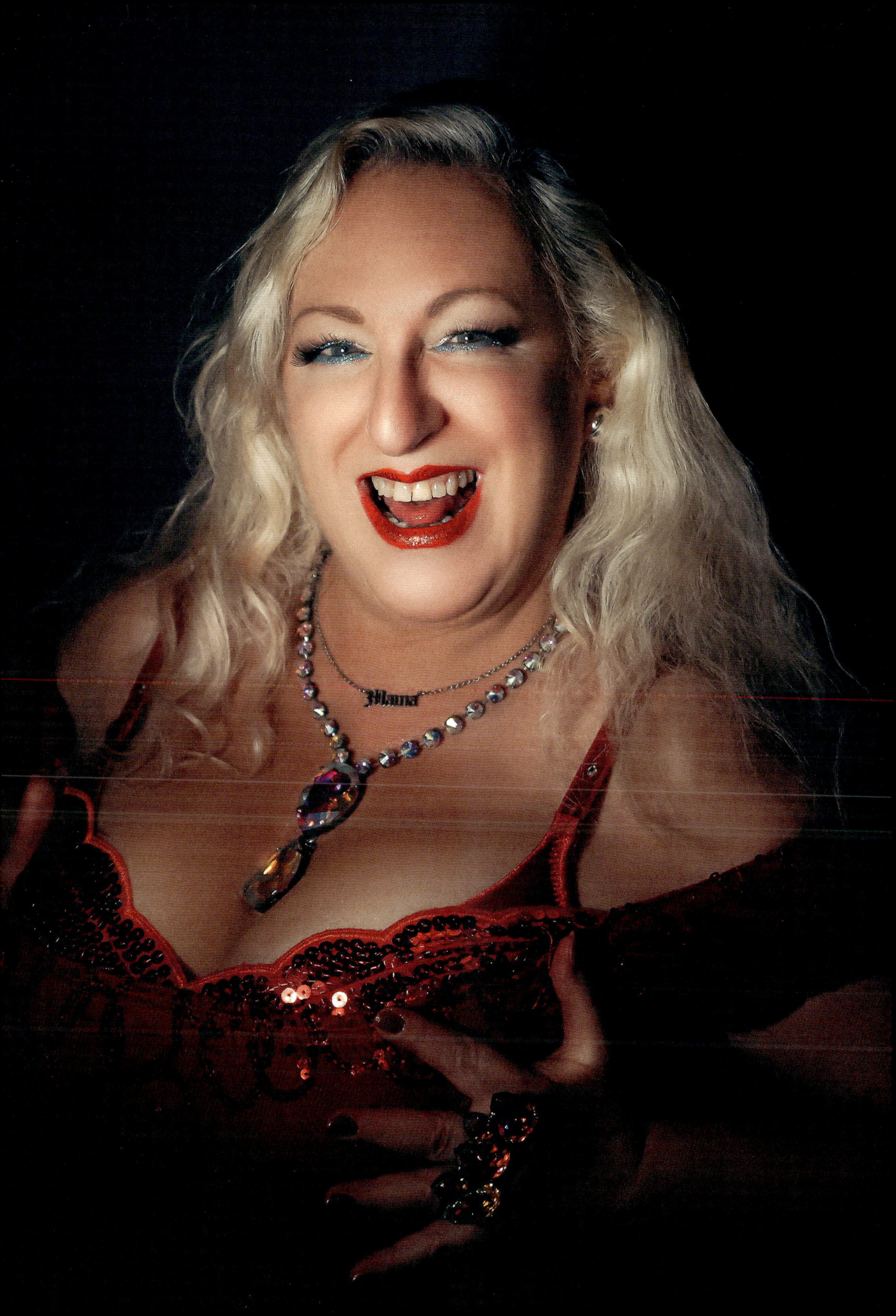

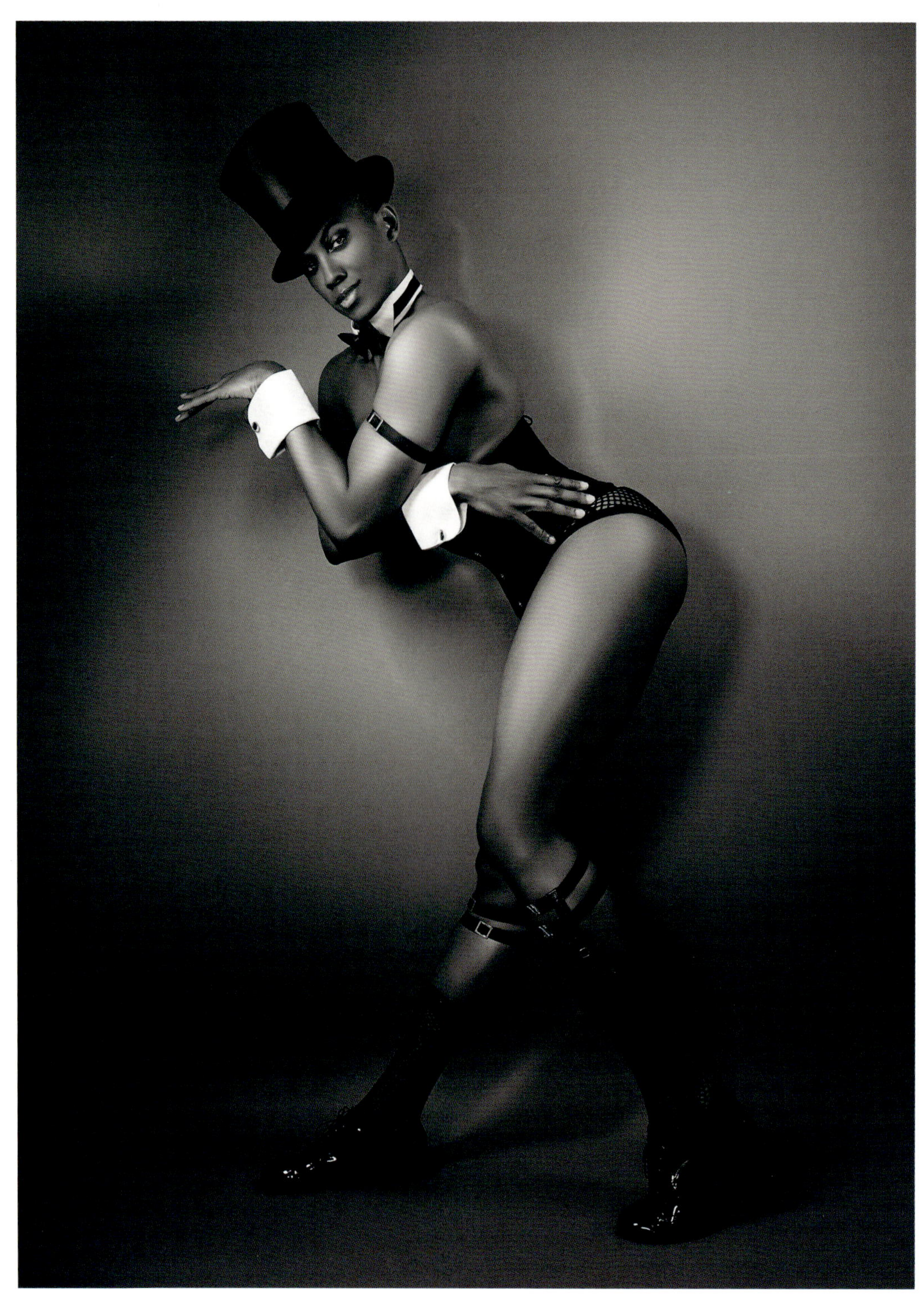


THE CHOCOLATE SHOWBOY
BURLESQUE

# THE BEAU BELLE BROTHERS
## BURLESQUE

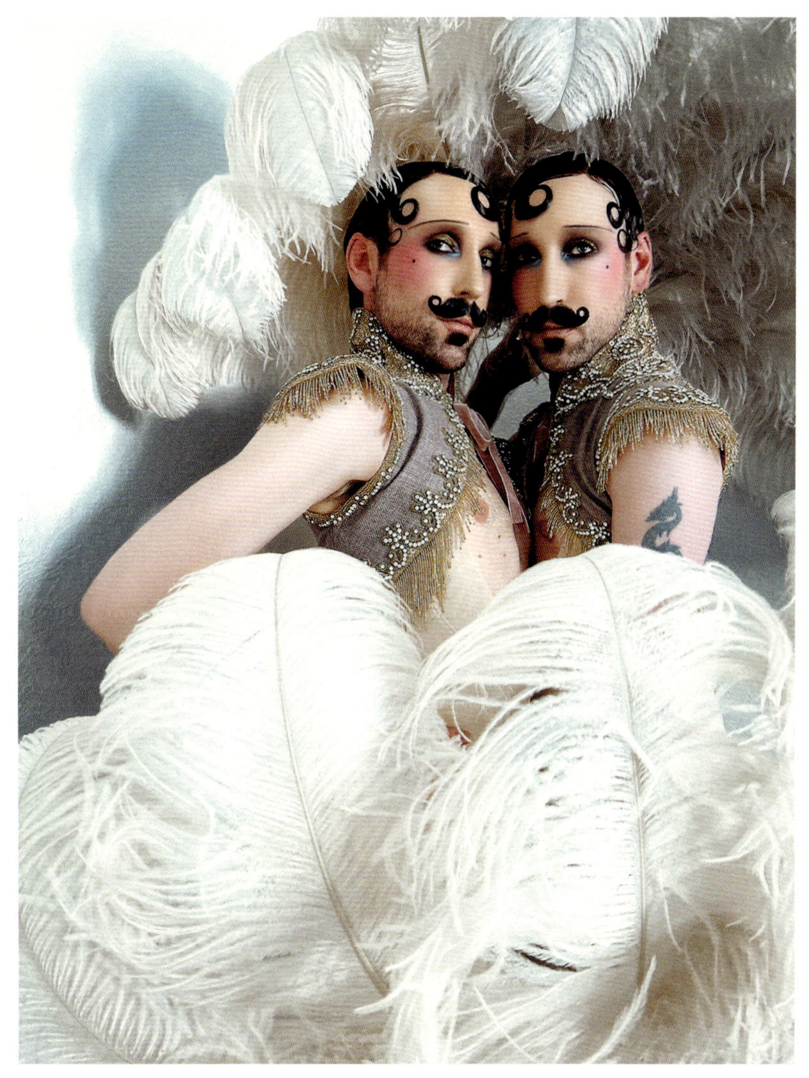

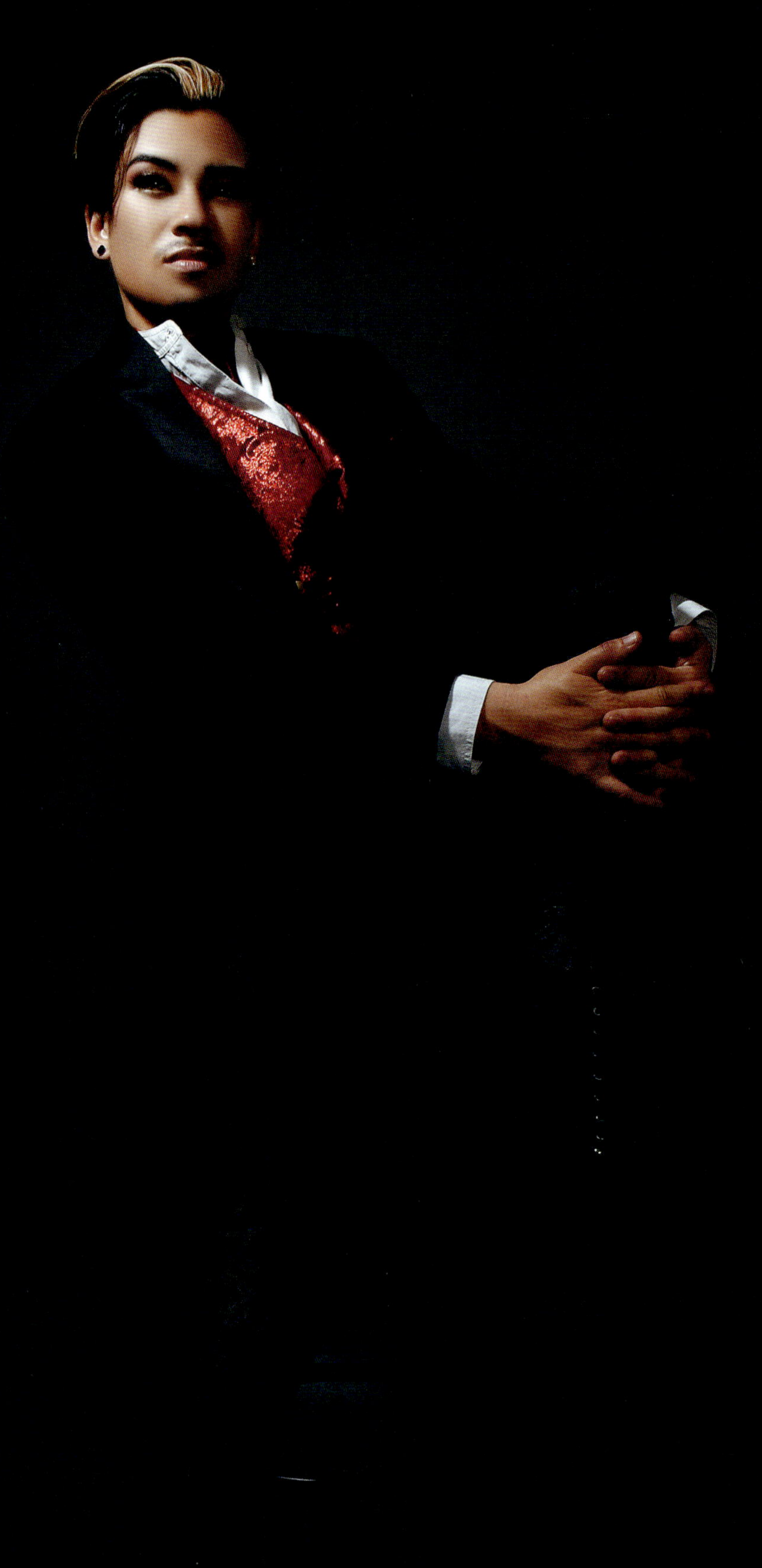

"I hope for more diversity, inclusivity, and intersectionality, and more producers who place all of the above at the forefront. I hope that the venues we perform in today stay, and more accessible trans and queer-run venues will open."

# SIGI MOONLIGHT

## DRAG KING

Like Ziggy Stardust, Sigi Moonlight is an extraterrestrial being brought to earth, an empty vessel who embodies different forms of masculinity to shine a light on its weird and terrifying extremes. Embodying characters from Charles Bronson to Old Asian Kung Fu Master and Captain Birdseye, Sigi mixes suave, sophisticated boylesque with character-based satire, taking traditionally dark masculine characters and turning them on their heads.

**"**A night at the cabaret for me is work. I'm focused on doing my job the best I can, but something happens to me when I get on stage that I can't quite explain. It's a version of myself that exists totally in the moment, free of all the fear and baggage I carry around in my day-to-day life.**"**

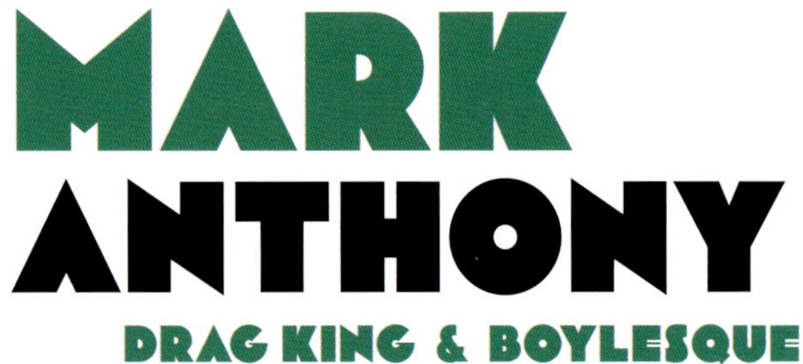

# MARK ANTHONY

## DRAG KING & BOYLESQUE

Mark Anthony is an award-winning Drag King and Boylesque performer on a mission to rhinestone masculinity and prove that anyone can be a heartthrob. Known for his suave, charismatic stage presence and detailed costuming, he is the producer of Quota Cabaret and holds the title of Mr Boylesque UK. He believes that joy and laughter are powerful tools of communication, and his acts play on a combination of nostalgia and masculine archetypes.

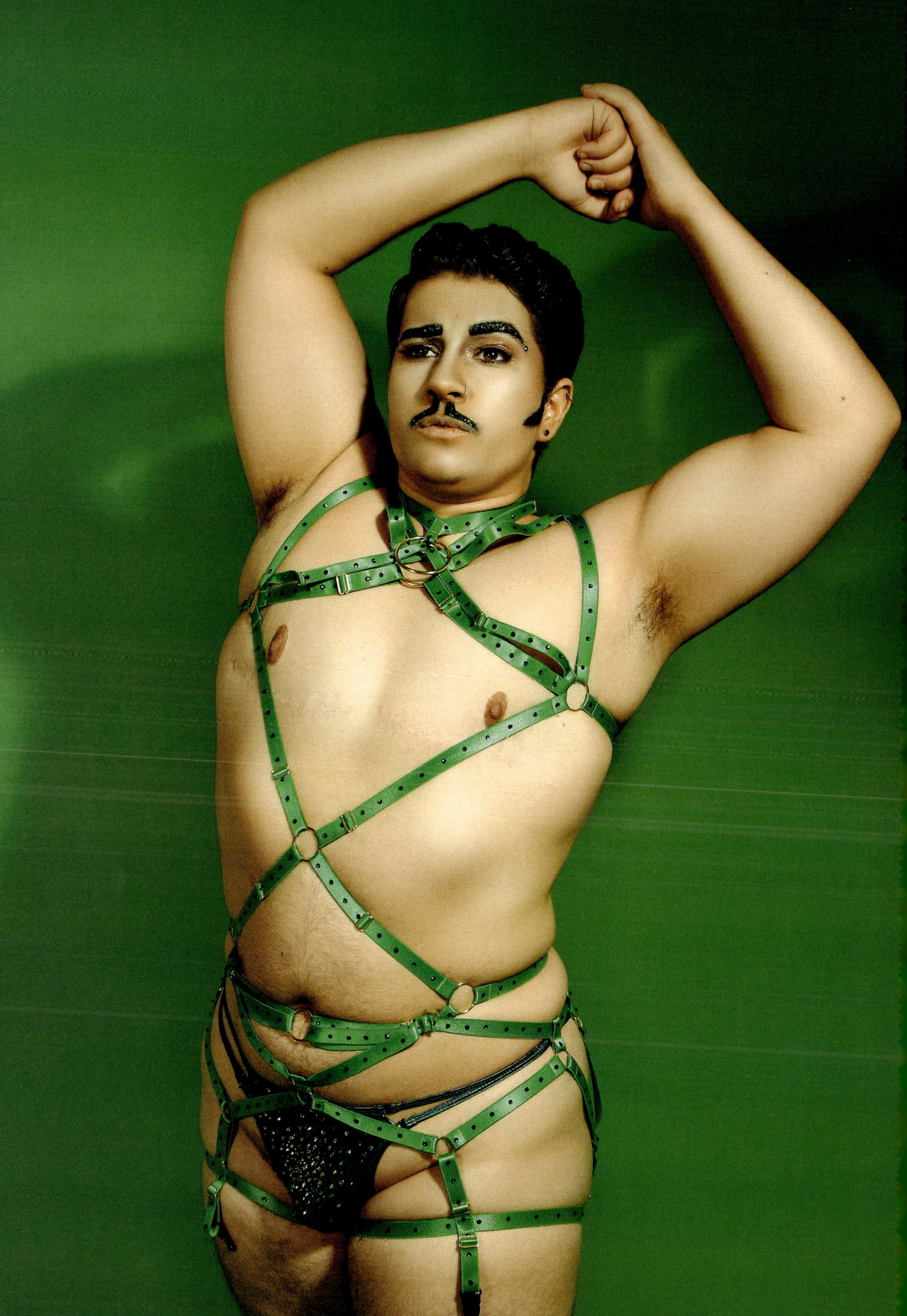

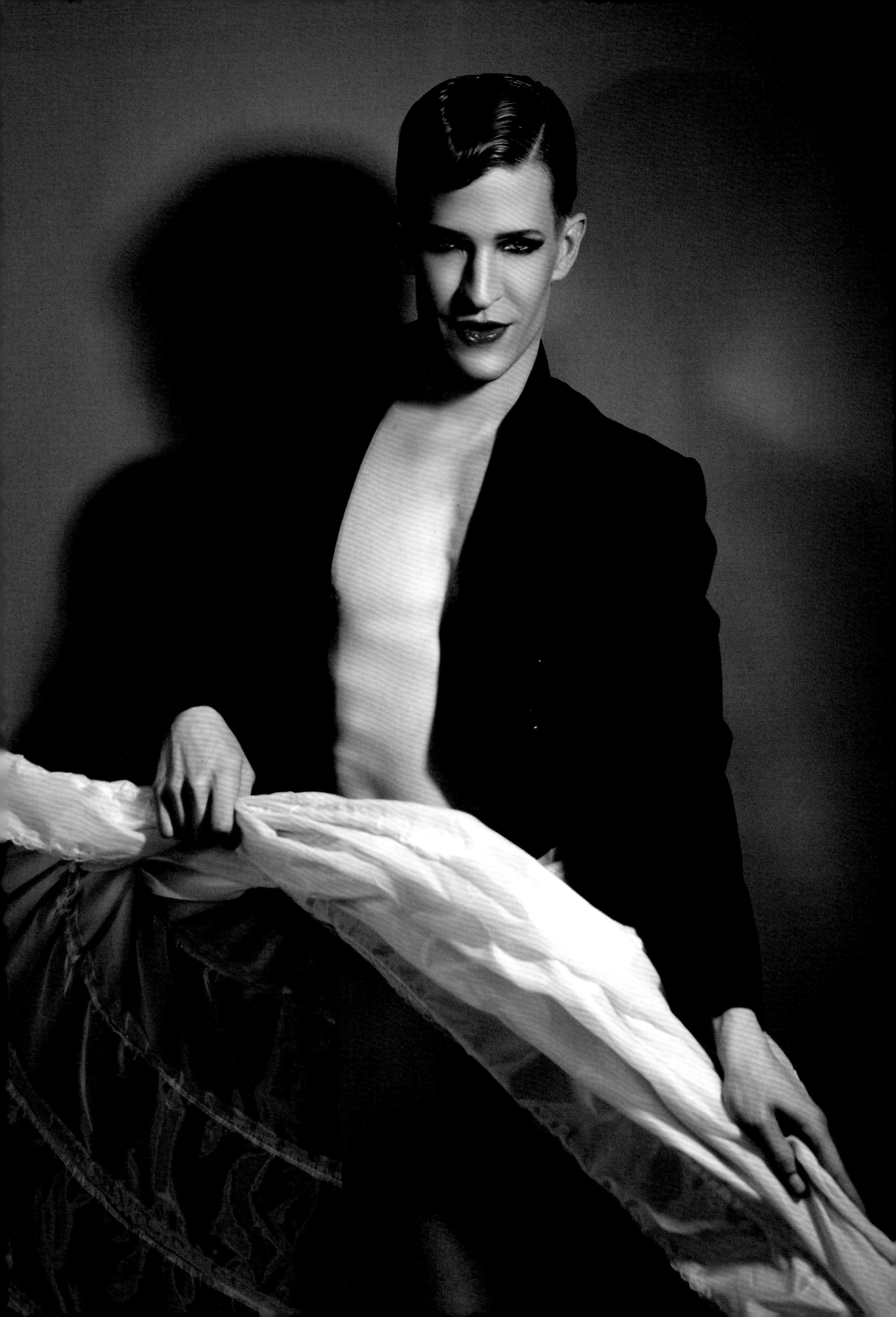

# LIFE AS A CABARET

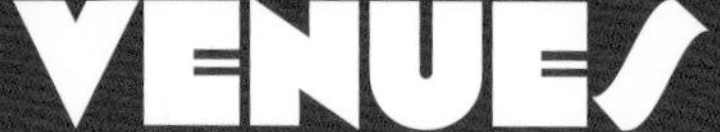


Initially, I intended to close this book with a list of all the cabaret venues in the UK. However, compiling such a list was not as simple as one might assume. Venues that cater exclusively to cabaret are extremely rare, with most queer and artistic venues always balancing precariously near closure. It is estimated that around a quarter of London's LGBTQ+ venues have closed in the last two decades, as well as many other cultural spaces. Very few venues are owned outright by those that operate them and are often threatened by gentrification, with the figures offered to landlords by developers being much more attractive than the rental income of artists. This trend was accelerated by the pandemic and the difficult economic landscape that followed.  In fact, as I write this, at least three cabaret venues in London and one in Manchester have closed their doors within the last few weeks.

It is very rare that a cabaret venue is offered protection. The Royal Vauxhall Tavern, possibly the UK's oldest continuously operating LGBTQ+ venue, has had to overcome several threats to survival. Opened as a LGBTQ+ venue in the 1950s (an exact date is difficult to pinpoint due to the oppressive anti-LGBTQ+ laws of the time), by the 1960s it was operating more or less openly as a community and entertainment space for queer people. In the 1980s it was famously a place of resistance to the homophobia that surrounded the HIV/AIDS crisis. In 1987, Lily Savage was on stage when hordes of policemen stormed the building and began arresting customers, wearing rubber gloves to protect themselves from the patrons. Before being arrested, she famously said through the microphone that the police were there to help with the washing up, and when later asked for her "real" name at the police station, she responded "Lily Veronica Mae Savage." The press that followed the raid and Lily's actions is said to have been a key turning point in public opinion and policing.

According to the memoirs of actress Cleo Rocos, Freddie Mercury once took Princess Diana to the Royal Vauxhall Tavern disguised as a Drag King. So much LGBTQ+ and cabaret history is held within its walls, but in the 1990s, it was nearly demolished by the local council to make way for a shopping centre, and in 2014, the venue was bought by developers and was again at risk of closure, this time possibly destined to be replaced by luxury flats. It was only saved after a passionate community campaign that saw it become the first LGBTQ+ building in the UK to be awarded Grade II listed status. This status now protects the Royal Vauxhall Tavern as a historic building.

There's an expression I've often heard repeated in dressing room chatter, that if there was ever an apocalypse, the only living things left would be cockroaches and cabaret performers. It's a reference to cabaret's resourcefulness, creativity, and adaptability. While venues are a precious resource, cabaret shows are, by necessity, not always linked to physical spaces. There are many across the country that move between venues, popping up in a city for one night or a few times a year. The Gilded Merkin has been producing shows since 2012 in Cardiff, Nottingham, and Birmingham, and The 100 Watt Club and Cheeky Devils Club cover much of South England. Hebden Bridge Burlesque Festival has been running since 2013, and there have been annual festivals in Leeds, Newcastle, Dundee, and Cork.

There are also shows and collectives operating all over the UK which represent performers who are often marginalised. The Cocoa Butter Club showcases and celebrates performers of colour, The Bitten Peach is an all-Asian cabaret collective, and the Enby Show platforms trans and non-binary performers. Homos and Houmous is an LGBT Jewish performance company, DisabiliTease platforms disabled performers, and the Invisible Cabaret aims to strip away stigma relating to mental health.

Cabaret is very much alive and well, despite all the challenges currently faced by the industry. Almost every major city in the UK has burlesque, drag, and cabaret scenes, and at least one regular show. Live performance can be accessed locally in almost every part of the country, you just have to look for it.

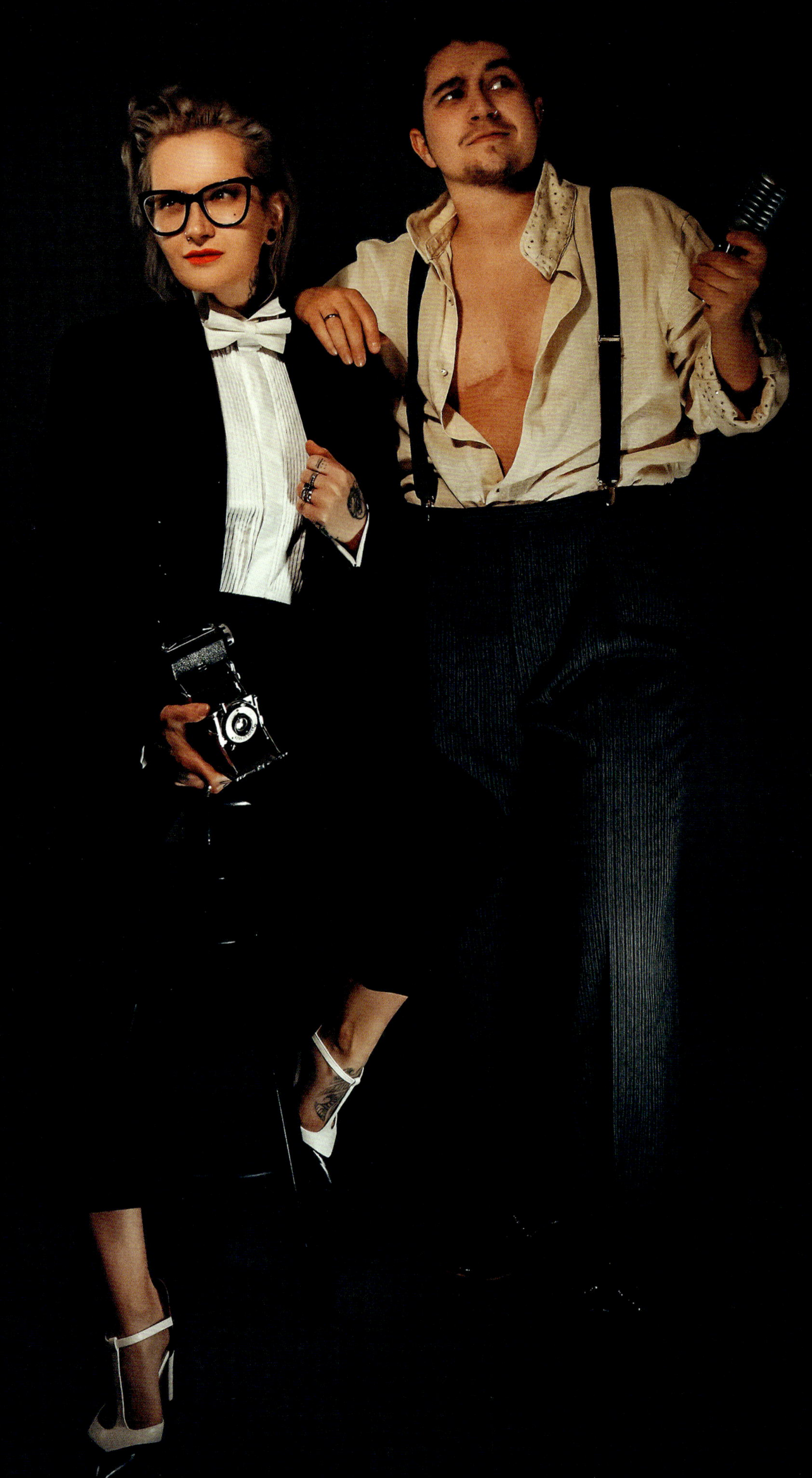

# VERONIKA MARX

began her career as a stylist and often showcased her love for the elegance and edge of the 1950s in her selections before becoming a photographer. She was one of few exclusive photographers selected for Dita Von Teese's GLAMONATRIX show and has worked with celebrity clients including burlesque queen Immodesty Blaze, Miss Miranda, Miss Tosh, Sabina Kelley, Tonia Buxton, and Kimberley Wyatt from The Pussy Cat Dolls, among others. Veronika's work has been featured in magazines such as Vintage Life Magazine, Bomb Boudoir, Slovakian OK Magazine, and she is the in-house photographer for Playboy Czech Republic.

# MARK ANTHONY

is a Drag King and Cabaret performer from the UK. After finishing an undergraduate degree at Oxford University and postgraduate study at Birkbeck College, University of London, Mark fell into drag through the LGBTQ+ community in London, and over the next seven years, thanks partly to a rare visual condition that hampered his ability to pursue other livelihoods, what began as a hobby turned into a full-time career. Mark now performs across the UK and internationally and is the reigning Mr Boylesque UK. He is proud to be the first trans-masculine performer to hold the Mr Boylesque title in any country and is keen to increase the visibility of trans/non-binary performers wherever possible. Through satire, nostalgia, music and burlesque, he hopes to pass on the feeling of empowerment that drag has given him, using it as a medium of social commentary about inequality, gender, identity, trans representation and queer joy.

I've got to give a shoutout to the real heroes of this book—the folks who let me capture their quirks and charm through the lens. You all are the stars of this show and without your cooperation, my camera would be as useful as a chocolate teapot. Also, to anyone who waltzed into my studio over the years, you've made it a hotbed of creativity and I owe you a heartfelt thank you.

Speaking of creativity, I want to express my gratitude to my partner in "writing" crime, Mark Anthony. He didn't just meet expectations; he blew them out of the water with a script that had me doing a happy dance. Mark, you're a legend in my book and I can't thank you enough. You are a genius.

Last but not least, a big shoutout to my husband, Steve. He's been the unsung hero enduring my artistic tantrums while still being my number one fan. Steve, you're a rockstar and I'm so lucky to have you in my corner.

To all of you—my wonderful subjects, my script sorcerer, and my ever-supportive hubby—thank you for adding your magic to this project. You've turned this book into something truly special, and I'm forever grateful.

Cheers to you all!

**VERONIKA MARX**

I would like to thank all the artists who have been photographed for the book, for trusting us with your images, art, and work. You inspire me, and I sincerely hope we've done you justice.

Thank you to Veronika for jumping into this project with both feet, for your tireless work to perfect every shot, for always listening to me and so beautifully capturing the community that I love.

Thank you to my fiancé Vi (Lilly SnatchDragon) for your unshakable belief in me, and never letting me doubt that my voice deserves to be heard, for taking part in the project and for moral support behind the scenes.

Thank you to my parents, Anna and Richard, and brother Adam for giving me the space to figure it all out and allowing your worldview to change with me, for always encouraging me to write, and for doing your best to support and understand my unconventional career path.

This book is dedicated to the cabaret community, to the queer and trans communities, and to everyone trying to make art outside of the mainstream, despite the many and varied boundaries they face.

**MARK ANTHONY**

LCCN: 2023920966
ISBN: 978-1-9519632-2-4

Printed and bound in China
First printing, 2024

**+ INFORMATION:**
For additional information
on our books and prints,
visit trope.com

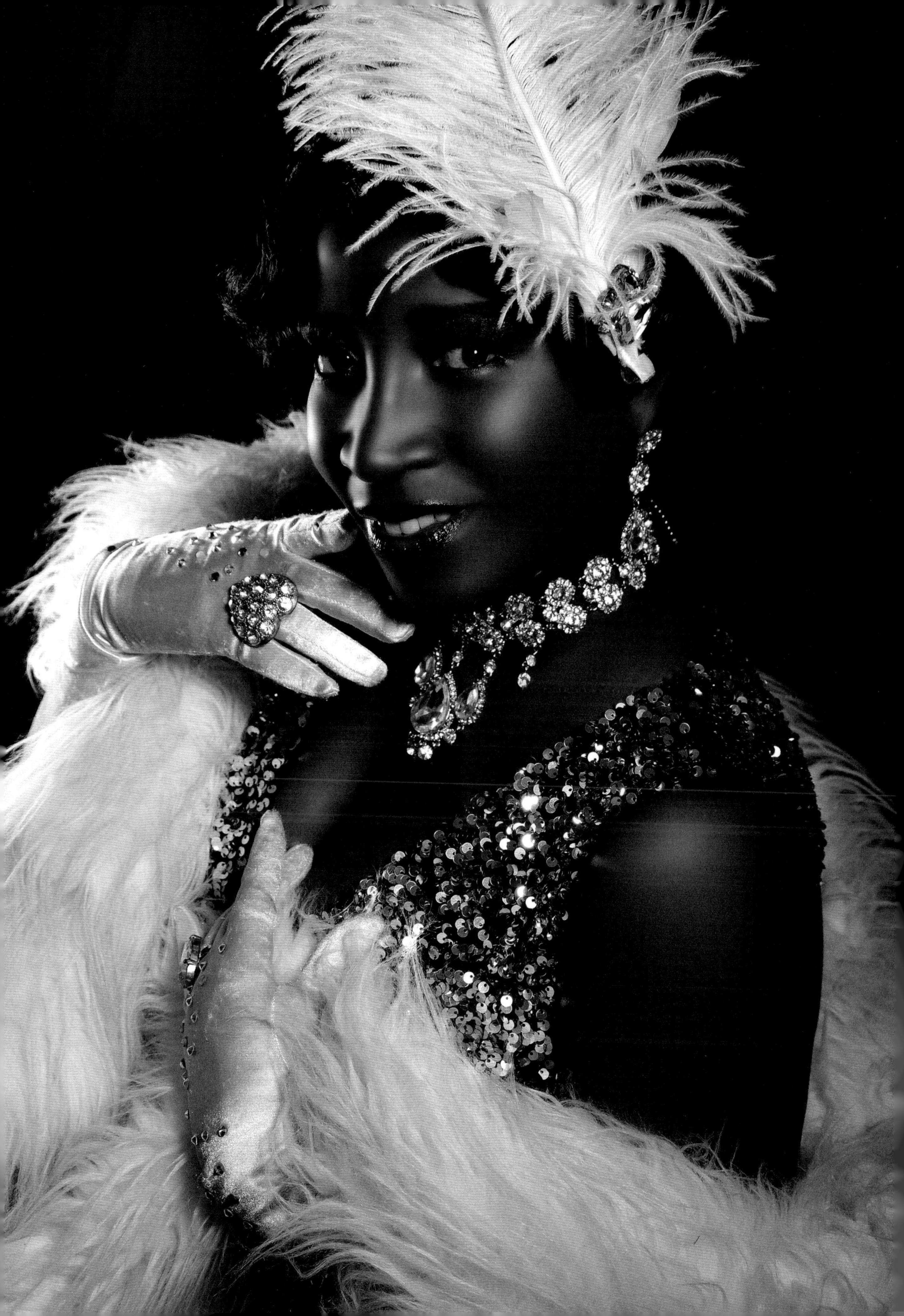